Sage & Smudge

The Ultimate Guide

by

Diane Ronngren

Published by ETC Publishing
Printed in the United States of America.

ISBN 978-1-930038-13-4

For requests and inquiries contact:
ETC Publishing
Reno, NV
www.etcpublishing.com

First Edition, First Printing 2003
15 14 13 12 11 10 3 4 5 6 7 8

Library of Congress Control Number 2003104511

Cover design by Gary Dunham

Concepts presented in this book derive from traditional European and American metaphysical and folk lore. They are not to be understood as directions, recommendations or prescriptions of any kind. Nor does the author or publisher make any claim to do more than provide information and report this lore.

This book is dedicated to
those who believed it should exist.
A special thanks to Kelly O'Tillery,
Donna Tokunaga, Gary Dunham
and my family for their
support and encouragement.

Table of Contents

Illustration by Dawn Mathews

Introduction

The White Sage Wand she is holding is about eight inches long and almost two inches around at its thickest point. The wand is tightly wrapped at the base with brightly colored thread. The thread has been wound in a pattern that continues up and around the Sage twigs and leaves, the entire length of the wand. It has helped to bind the Sage leaves firmly in place as they dried.

She holds that brightly bound base of her wand now firmly in her left hand as she lights the top of it with her lighter and watches the flames burn hungrily for a few moments as they ignite the dried White Sage. Then the flames recede to an even glow, as the Sage wand and she become ready to do the clearing work. Smoke rises from the wand into the air with every move she makes - dancing with the movement of the air in the doorway where she is standing.

Placing the lighter in the pocket of her vest, she picks up a small ceramic bowl. She will use it to catch any ash that might fall from the wand during the process of her clearing ceremony. She glances quickly around to check that the matching ceramic pot with sand in it is placed outside the entrance-way to the room she is about to clear. And then she turns her attention to the process of clearing her personal space.

As you read this introduction to a Sage and Smudge ritual, you have an image of a woman who is about to take charge of the energy in her environment, to clear it from any negativity, and to call in supportive and helpful spirits (angels or other spiritual essences or representations she believes in) to clear, protect and heal her personal space. In a way, you are "watching" someone involved in "active prayer". This is the most common way individuals use the process of their personal Sage and Smudge Rituals - to talk to their God, the Essence of Good they believe in, and ask for support and protection in the course of their daily lives.

The use of herbs for healing and to enhance well-being was a common practice in the past, and still is part of the lives of many people in every culture today. Burning herbs for their pleasant aroma is a very ancient practice. Down through the ages man and women have sought to call the attention of their gods to an offering or a prayer they make. The image of smoke rising towards the heavens is symbolic of their prayers rising to the ears of their gods.

In ancient Babylon, in the temples of Egypt, in the various Mediterranean religious centers, in Ancient Greek and Roman religious ceremonies, in the days of Abraham and the prophets of the Bible and the wandering tribes of Israel, among the Celts and the Ancient Britons and the Vikings, people burned offerings to their gods. All believed that the smoke rising into the heavens called these gods' attention to the prayers of their believers. In other parts of the world, China, North and South America, Africa, India- each culture had its rituals and ceremonies, and each of them believed in the power of sacred smoke to lift their prayers into the heavens.

Our own culture has its roots in these ancient customs and the beliefs that were carried from one part of our world to another by the powerful nations and religions of the past. Each time a nation met another nation, whether for purposes of battle or trade, they came into contact with each other's beliefs. Prayers, blessings and offerings were observed; customs and practices of the different societies and individuals were tested by each. Any parts that fit with what either society believed were incorporated into their own practices, eventually becomming part of their ceremonies and rituals.

In our times, the use of burning incense, or smoke rising from the altar in some form, is still part of all of the major religions' practices. Many other less mainstream spiritual groups have incorporated the use of herbs in various ways into their practices, their rituals and ceremonies. Even those who do not follow a particular form of religious observance enjoy the customs of the culture they live in, the herbs and the scent of the "perfumes" of our earth. Many "pray" in their own way, or wish, or hope or believe that some form of positive thinking can help create the future they envision.

Use this book like you would any guidebook, to create your own sacred smoke rituals. You will find tips on how to select Sage and Smudge herbs and a variety of sacred smoke "tools" commonly used in personal ceremonies and rituals. Use all of this information to enhance your spiritual and metaphysical connection to your Universe, to the Power you believe in.

Find out how to cleanse negative energy and clear your personal space. Heal your relationship to the world you live in and share with those you love. Use any of the ceremonies described in this book to enhance your own focus on the issues in your life, on your "prayers", your vision, your hopes and your wishes. Empower yourself by creating your own rituals and ceremonies as you become more familiar with the benefit of personal Sage and Smudge rituals for clearing and healing your personal space.

Remember that all ritual and ceremony helps us examine our beliefs, to explore the possibilities of our journey on earth and the fears that stop us from becoming all we can be. They help us visualize the lives we want to live, and to understand our connection to the Whole. The very process of carrying out a ritual or participating in a ceremony is your response to an invitation to visit the place of spirit, of vision, of the creative force within - to share a moment with the Creator.

Enjoy the journey!

Diane Ronngren

Chapter 1

Sacred Smoke

For thousands of years herbs have been used to bring healing, to enhance the flavors of the foods we eat, to improve general physical well-being, and in rituals of all kinds. These rituals over time became part of the culture, tradition and lore brought down to us via our ancestors. In every society, every culture, every country, people have customarily found the roots, stems, sap, oils, leaves, buds, flowers and seeds of the trees and plants growing in their native soil useful both in very practical ways in their daily lives, and on a spiritual level. It was common then to believe that if something was valuable to mankind on earth, it would also be valuable to the gods they worshipped.

People identified the essences of the various plants, and used them quite naturally in their religious and spiritual quest for connection to a Higher Power. In ancient times, centers of religious and spiritual activity were also places of healing and medical treatment for all kinds of ills. And in the temples of ancient times, burning offerings and herbs were often part of the ceremonial aspect of spiritual healing that accompanied the more practical process of physical healing.

Sacred smoke itself is common as a means of connecting people to their spiritual source. Not only did the ancient religions of the past commonly include sacred smoke in their rituals, today's followers of the "western" traditions of the Greek Orthodox, Catholic and some Protestant Churches have candles and/or incense burning during religious services. The smoke (or smudge) that rises symbolizes prayers rising towards the heavens.

Outside Buddhist temples in the east you will see collections of hundreds of smoking, individual sticks of incense placed in special urns or holders outside of the temples, the sacred smoke rising to the heavens, and filling the air with a pungent scent. Worshippers stop to breathe the fragrant air of the temple, to light another stick of incense to add to the already numerous ones burning there, or to cup their hands with the smoke that is rising all around, and draw it to their body with their cupped hands, to purify themselves before going into a temple.

Smudging, the burning of herbs to create aromatic, sacred smoke, is one of the most frequently observed ritual acts in the Native American tradition. Smudging with Sage and other dried herbs to clear and purify space, people or objects, or for religious and spiritual purposes outside a church, temple or holy place is a Native American tradition. Nearly every Native American ceremony integrates some form of smudging. The Native American purification ceremony is similar in essence to ones carried out in a wide variety of traditional religious celebrations in other cultures all over the world.

In all of these religious and spiritual ceremonies, the smoke rising from the incense or the smoldering herbs serves as an action that focuses the consciousness of the participants inward. It is meant to help the participants stay intent on their thoughts and concerns, their prayers about what they want to be accomplished through the ceremony or ritual in which they are involved. The smoke rising from the herbs during a ritual is also believed to symbolize the power of good to drive off or diffuse evil spirits and negative influences, to purify, cleanse and heal the spiritual and emotional, the conscious and unconscious (even sometimes the physical) being of the people who are taking part in the ceremony!

North American Indians most frequently use different varieties of Sage and Sagebrush, Cedar or Juniper, Sweet Grass and Tobacco in their sacred ceremonies. These herbs are commonly burned either separately, or in combination with one another. Traditionally the loose herbs are either tossed on a flame or a very hot surface - or they are placed in a shell or fire tolerant container before being lit. Then the herbs are allowed to burn, to "smudge", filling the space with aromatic smoke.

While Sage wands and loose Sage leaves are very often used on their own in modern Sage and Smudge rituals, some other dried herbs and herbal combinations with Sage have also gained a considerable level of popularity in the sacred smoke ceremonies of today. It is not unusual to find smudge wands or sticks (or bundles) in the marketplace combining Sage and Lavender, Sage and Cedar, Sage and Juniper, Sage and Sweet Grass. You can buy wands, sticks or bundles with a combination of either Sagebrush or Sage leaves and one or more of these other herbs.

Sometimes the Sage and other herbs are bound singly or combined, pressed together to form the shape of a "stick" or "wand", and tied with thread or string to bind the herbs in place. These "Sage Wands" (as they are commonly called today) can then be carried around a space, moved around an individual, a group of people or a ritual article that is the focus of the ceremony.

It is also not uncommon for people who are carrying out modern-day aromatic sacred smoke ceremonies - cleansing, clearing or energy healing rituals - to combine loose sage leaves with other dried loose herbs. Many believe that burning two or more of the herbs simultaneously is a powerful way to combine the energy of the different herbs in the ceremony, ritual or process they are performing. You will find people using dried White Sage leaves and Mugwort, Cedar, Sweetgrass, or Tobacco (powder or leaf form) from the Native American tradition of the Shamans and people of North and South America. And it is also common to find people combining Sage with Juniper, Lavender, Rosemary or Thyme to create modern day aromatic smoke rituals and ceremonies in accordance with the ancient religions and traditions of their forefathers from other parts of the world.

Our connection to the past and our understanding of how we can benefit from personalized sacred smoke rituals can be traced to the cultural traditions of our ancestors who valued the plants we commonly use today in our own lives, in our culinary creations, and in other ways in our environment. Now, more often than not, using these herbs to heal our personal space in a spiritual way is becoming as popular as using them for culinary, decorative or medicinal purposes!

Our modern-day practice of using Sage (or Sage combined with other dried herbs) in personal smudging rituals and ceremonies is based on a combination of the spiritual, medicinal, herbal and cultural teachings of the past. These teachings and customs have been collected from many cultures and combined in this book to provide information about how you can carry out Sage and Smudge Rituals for personal clearing and healing today.

Sage

Desert Sage

The roots of the use of Sage as a medicinal herb can be found in many cultures from around the world. The Latin name for this herb, "Salvia", can be translated: "to be saved". In the Middle Ages in Britain it was sometimes believed that the plant could "render immortality", according to the 17th Century writings of John Evelyn. And, if that didn't work, well, then one could plant Sage near the graves of the deceased, to ensure that the death would lead to salvation in heaven!

The ancient Romans used Sage in their public bath houses to soothe aching muscles and tired feet, something very important to a people who marched and built roads to connect their Empire via a network of highways! In many parts of the world, Sage was eaten or immersed in hot water to form a kind of "tea". Many cultures believed Sage could fortify the body and give it strength, and it was believed to promote longevity.

Over the centuries Sage has been used as a "beauty product" in many cultures - particularly as an astringent, to treat different skin problems; it was also used as both a shampoo and to dye hair black! Sage has been served as a culinary enhancement to certain foods because it is said to aid digestion. For the same reason, it has been offered as a savory at the end of a meal (and in some cultures it was considered useful for treating the difficult symptoms of dysentery).

Sage has served as an antiseptic, a mouth wash, and to treat wounds of various kinds, burns or insect bites. It has long been believed to reduce perspiration, salivation, lactation - any kind of fluid secretion. And it has been used successfully by women during menopause to treat hot sweats!

In China "Sage Tea" became a popular beverage for calming the nerves. At one time China and Holland were involved in trade with one another, the Chinese trading three times the weight of tea for Sage leaves. The American Indians used Sage baths to reduce fevers, and some of them made a salve of the dried and powdered leaves mixed with grease to treat skin disorders or sores.

Even in modern times, this herb has been studied for its medicinal applications. Scientists at the Nippon Roche Research Center in Kamakura, Japan (in the Department of Microbiology and Chemotherapy) have said that powdered Sage or Sage tea helps to prevent blood clots from forming. They have found that Sage can be used in the prevention and treatment of myocardial infarction, or to treat non-specific coronary pain.

Most cultures used Sage as an herb in their food or drink, or externally as a bath or a salve to treat various physical conditions-or to prevent them. However, upon the arrival of the Europeans to North America, they observed that the native peoples of the continent used Sage in their spiritual rituals, to create an aromatic, sacred smoke.

Smudging with Sage and other dried herbs to clear and purify space, people or objects, or for religious and spiritual purposes outside a church, temple or holy place is a Native American tradition. Sage is associated with "purity". The smudge from the burning Sage alone (or in combination with other herbs) in Native American healing rituals is used to clear and purify a space. The sacred smoke from Sage is thought to "consecrate" (sanctify or make "holy") the person, place or thing that is the focus of the ceremony. Sage smudge clears any negativity surrounding the people who are participating in a ceremony, and cleanses objects of negative energy or "bad medicine". The original meaning of the smudging ritual was that the rising smoke carried the requests of the Native American people to the Great Spirit they believed in, to the Spirit of the Air.

White Sage

In smudging - the ritual burning of herbs - the aromatic "smoke" from the herbs is used to alter, cleanse or purify the energy in a specific space. Native American rituals can consist of brief, barely 10-minute-long Sage and Smudge ceremonies where a burning piece of Sage, Cedar or other plant is the tool used to create sacred smoke. Or a Sage and Smudge ritual may be part of a very intense up to 10-day-long ceremony involving spoken formulas, the singing of sacred songs, and participation in a "sweat lodge". These longer ceremonies often include other specific and traditional diet, sexual or physical requirements.

The Native American Indians associate Sage or Sagebrush with "purity" and the spirits of the heavens. During traditional dances, dancers might wear wreaths of Sage on their heads, or chew on the leaves, as well as using the dried leaves and twigs to create aromatic, sacred smoke during their religious observations.

CEDAR

In the Cherokee tradition, Cedar is often used in smudging rituals, with or without Sage. Cedar is believed to be very effective in dispelling negative energy. According to tradition, breathing the smoke from the burning wood, bark or needles of the Cedar tree helps people to make personal choices that benefit the highest good of all. The smoke from burning Cedar is believed to dissipate fear and anxiety, and help us to know that the really important thing about any experience in life is to learn from the consequences of our

choices. Hence, Cedar gives us courage, and teaches us to trust in our willingness to grow in wisdom.

Usually the needles from the Cedar tree are used in a Sage and Smudge ritual, or the small twigs with the needles still attached are bound together with White Sage or Sagebrush to create a wand. You can easily find this type of wand in the marketplace today. It is less common now for people to burn the wood or bark from the Cedar tree in their rituals. The easiest way to use the needles themselves, is to toss dry needles onto a fire along with other herbs you have chosen for your own purposes.

Sweet Grass

Sweet Grass is very commonly used in the North American Indian tribal ceremonies, and has a fresh, clean smell, something like newly-mown hay. It is most commonly braided into the form of a stick or wand. It is believed burning Sweet Grass will drive away negative thoughts and fear of the unknown. It is also believed to have the ability to clear and remove negative energy from a person or a space. Sweet Grass is often used in Sweat Lodge ceremonies, or in healing ceremonies and other purification rituals performed by the Native Americans in North America.

Tobacco

TOBACCO.

Tobacco is a purely North American herb which was introduced to European traders by the native peoples of the land who welcomed them when they arrived to settle. They, in turn, introduced it to the rest of the world. Whether burning, smoking, chewing, drinking its juice or using it to make a protective ointment, Tobacco was regarded with special reverence by the elders of the Native American Indian tribes because they believed that it could bring peace and understanding between people with different perspectives. They shared it in the form of sacred smoke on special occasions as a sign of hospitality and brotherhood.

The Native American Indians shared peace pipes with the first European settlers, which introduced them to the habit of smoking dried Tobacco. The Native Americans themselves traditionally smoked Tobacco more for magic, shamanic or purification purposes than for enjoyment. When smoking these peace pipes or using the herb for ceremonial purposes, smoke was first blown or wafted towards the four corners of the world at the commencement of a ritual.

When, or if, you are going to use Tobacco in a smudge ceremony, you can use it either in its leaf form (the leaves can also be bound together to dry and thus build a "wand"), or as a powder. The loose powder form or loosely crushed dry leaves of the herb can be used in the same way you might use Cedar needles, by throwing it on a smoldering flame or into a fire to create sacred smoke. Follow the Native American tradition when using this herb for ceremonial purposes, and waft the smoke in the four directions, North, East, South and West before continuing with your ritual.

JUNIPER

Juniper is a very popular addition to a Sage wand, stick or bundle. Its addition to the Sage stick or wand creates an aromatic smoke. If the berries and the small branches (or twigs) are included in the wand, the oils from these parts of the plant increase the heat and the amount of smoke, as well as the length of the time the wand will burn or "smudge".

The tradition is that Juniper provides a powerful protective energy, and in ancient times it was carried in a pouch worn inside the clothing or in a pocket for that very reason! On its own, burning Juniper wood or bark gives off only a minimally visible but highly aromatic smoke. In fact, in ancient times smoke from burning Juniper wood was used in the ritual purification of temples. The Juniper smoke was believed to aid clairvoyance, and stimulate contact with the "Other-world" of spirits. It is said that the Central Europeans used the smoke from the burning Juniper wood as part of their spring-time cleansing rituals. The Celts burned Juniper at their autumn Samhain Fire Festival to celebrate the beginning of the Celtic "New Year". The healing and disinfectant powers of Juniper were widely respected in the Middle Ages, and Juniper smoke would be used to fumigate homes where the occupant had died of a communicable disease.

One of the most popular uses of Juniper today is as a flavoring in gin. The berries of the Juniper tree are dried and crushed, much like we would do with a peppercorn, or they are pressed for their juice. In fact, the use of this herb as a culinary spice or flavoring is a very ancient one. It was widely used as a spice (often dried and ground) in England and Scotland to give flavor to sauces or game dishes. In mediaeval times the berries were used to flavor whisky in Scotland - probably to make them sufficiently palatable to ingest for their healing properties!

The earliest written records describing the medicinal use of Juniper berries are recorded in an Egyptian papyrus dating back to 1500 BC - where it was suggested as a cure for tapeworm infestations. The oil from the plant has been used for everything from the treatment of flatulence (for which it is still used today), to abortion or treating a woman following a miscarriage or difficult birth.

LAVENDER

Lavender is one extremely popular addition to a Sage bundle, Sage stick or wand. The historical use of Lavender goes back to the time of the early Egyptians who wrapped their dead in shrouds dipped in a perfume made from the

plant. Lavender was valued as a perfume by many cultures surrounding the Mediterranean, and is believed to have been spread through Europe by the sea-faring Greeks around 600 B.C. Europeans have loved the scent ever since. Romans, male and female, so valued the scent that they used Lavender oils for bathing, cooking and scenting the air, much as we use a room deodorizer today in our personal environments.

Lavender was not only valued for its scent in ancient times, but also for its healing and medicinal qualities. For example, during the Great Plague in London in the 17th Century, people believed that if they had a bouquet of Lavender attached to their wrist, they wouldn't contract the deadly disease! Indeed, it was firmly believed by most of the ancient cultures that Lavender could heal all kinds of illnesses, and it had the ability to dispel "dark humors", an affliction of the spirit we would likely identify today as "depression".

Lavender has long been believed to protect against the "evil eye", and it has been used as a protective agent against physical and spiritual harm. But historically it has also been valued as a powerful "tool" for spiritual or psychic enhancement as well, helping to make dreams and wishes come true! It has been used to facilitate divination or clairvoyant dreaming. But mostly it has been valued down through the centuries for its relaxation and sleep benefit.

Lavender is famous for its soothing and relaxing qualities, and even today it is used to treat hyperactivity and insomnia. It is also used to treat a wide range of physical symptoms such as flatulence, bacterial infection, and gum disease. In an environmental context, in both ancient and modern times, Lavender has been recommended as an agent to destroy airborne molds. Many of the members of the European Royal families have, down through the ages, demanded that their pillows be filled with Lavender! Queen Elizabeth II uses products from the famous Lavender company, "Yardly and Co." of London, as did her namesake, Elizabeth I.

Today many people place Lavender inside their pillows to enhance their sleep at night, or they have a bunch of Lavender in a vase in their bedroom. Sometimes people place Lavender among their underclothes, in their drawers and closets, or in other places where clothing is stored, so that when they wear the clothing they will feel "relaxed" and less "stressed out" by the daily challenges they face. The essence of the plant is believed to be so powerful that if (or when) you are depressed, one whiff of the scent will alleviate all sorrow, and you will be filled with joyous feelings!

If you use a wand, stick or bundle that includes both Sage and Lavender, you will find the scent of the herbs quite pleasant and relaxing, no matter what reason you have for burning them! Creating sacred smoke with such a tool helps to enhance the process of achieving a peaceful atmosphere or environment in any area of your personal world.

Mugwort

Similar to both Juniper and Lavender, European and Mediterranean cultures recognized Mugwort as a healing herb, and it was greatly valued for its essence. People believed that Mugwort could protect them from "evil spirits" - especially while they were sleeping. So they often placed it inside pillows or in their beds to protect them while they were sleeping. And if they were out traveling, they would bring Mugwort along with them to place in the beds or places where they would sleep along the journey. This is how the herb reached North America; it was brought by the European pilgrims who settled the country. They planted it near their homes in order to have ready access to it for their needs. Over time it has spread across many parts of the country, and today it can be found growing wild in nature in the soil of its new home.

The virtues and powers associated with this plant, according to the literature are: protection from all forms of evil (including poison), strength, psychic powers, prophetic dreams, emotional and psychological healing, and astral projection. The Greeks and Romans associated the plant with the planet "Artemis" (hence its Latin name: Artemesia vulgarus). The Roman name for this planet (in Greek: Artemesia) is the same one we use today - "Venus". They also associated the plant's powers with their goddess,

Diana, the Huntress. Dried Mugwort can be placed in pillows or among bedclothing to enhance relaxation and dreaming. When it is burned to create aromatic sacred smoke, or infused and drunk as a tea, Mugwort is said to bring clarity and the ability to see and speak of the future.

Rosemary

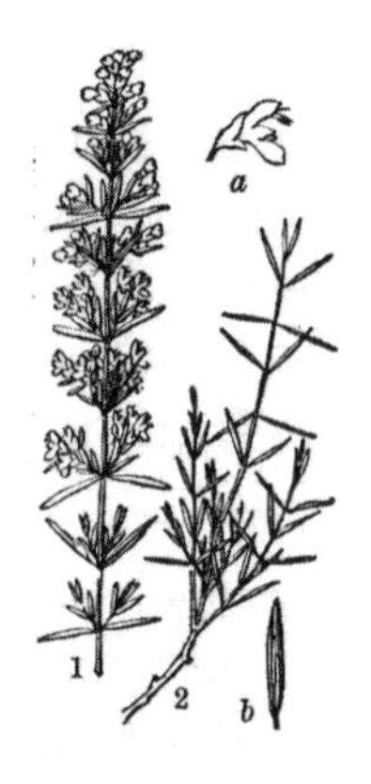

Today we find this herb most commonly used as a culinary flavoring, like a spice for sausage, one used to add flavor to meat dishes (particularly lamb), fowl and fish. Some use Rosemary to enhance the taste of stuffed vegetables, vinegars and wine, or drinks like lemonade and ale. Rosemary has a long history of use as an herbal medicine, and has over the years been prescribed by healers for everything from headache and toothache to curing baldness or rheumatism. You can find it as an ingredient in practical things like soaps, lotions or creams, and it is a much enjoyed herb found in sachets and potpourris used to perfume areas in people's personal environments, like the bathroom, or the entrance area of a home.

However, the history of Rosemary reveals a very strong spiritual and religious connection. It is, in fact, one of the most ancient sacred smoke herbs, and was burned at temples and shrines in Ancient Greece to drive away evil spirits. It was even used in the hospitals of the time (which were located near the temples) to drive away illnesses from the patients being cared for there. It is said that the

Pharaohs of Egypt placed Rosemary branches in their tombs to remind them of their former life. Ever since, Rosemary has been the herb people carried with them when they visited the sick or attended funerals - partly because of the strong scent and partly for the same reason we might put on a surgical mask to avoid catching germs from someone who is ill - to protect from infection!

It became a custom to drop sprigs of Rosemary onto a coffin as a kind of "promise" that people would not forget their loved one who had died. And, over time it became a tradition to use Rosemary as a "reminder" in a variety of social contexts. Sprigs would be placed in bridal bouquets, or in the corsage worn by the groom, so neither would forget their vows, and would remember to remain faithful to one another. In some countries, unmarried women who wanted to know whom they would marry, would place Rosemary under their pillow, to dream of their future husband.

Including Rosemary with Sage and other herbs in a wand, stick or bundle, or using it on its own (or with other loose herbs) to burn in a holder to create aromatic smoke represents a desire to "remember" someone, or some former time in your life. It can also be a burned to attract friendship and love or to enhance good interactions between people, for healing from sadness, for seeking protection in some difficult situation or to drive away nightmares or fears.

Thyme

Thyme is another of the sacred smoke herbs that were brought to North America by the Pilgrims. It was the herb

they used to preserve food (especially meats, cheeses, fat and oil) for the long journey from Europe. It was also the answer of the time for treating most infectious diseases, and it was highly valued for its disinfectant and healing properties. Once planted in the soil of its new home Thyme thrived and spread across the country with the waves of settlers - all needing to preserve the food they brought with them for the long journey.

The history of the use of Thyme goes way back into the annals of time in several major cultural traditions. It was used (as a preservative) in the funeral industry of Ancient Egypt. Since then it has served as an herb used at funerals to assure an easy passage into the "afterlife" and it is one of the herbs still commonly used in embalming. The ancient Greeks were very familiar with the herb, and it was there that Thyme was most used in sacred smoke rituals of various kinds, as a religious incense.

It was considered to be such a powerful herb, that it was burned first, prior to other offerings, to purify both the altar itself and those who would participate in the ceremony. It was believed to restore vigor and intellectual acuity to the mind, to guard against infertility, to protect people and homes from attacks or illness, to give courage so people were willing to face the challenges of life as they arose, and to preserve and protect the wealth, health and strength of the community from outside danger of any kind.

The third source of mythology and folklore associated with this herb comes from the British Isles. People there believed that the matted, knotted and twisted branches of Thyme in the garden provided a home for the "Faery Folk" - whose job it was to make sure that the garden grew, that the bees found nectar and made honey, and that the earth provided abundance to the people who lived and shared those riches. Indeed, one source promises, "If you wash your eyes with the dew from the leaves of Thyme before the sun rises on May 1st, you can see the fairies just at the moment of first light."

Today, while it is most commonly used as a culinary herb, it has many other uses both as a pharmaceutical ingredient and as a component in over-the-counter cures of various kinds - and is often mentioned in the context of antioxidants.

Thyme can be included in a Sage wand, stick or bunch, or burned on its own, as it was in ancient rituals. It is best used at times when a "rite of passage" is celebrated, to indicate that an individual is moving from one stage to another in their life. It is also recommended for calling on energy to support courage, to ask for protection, and to experience a feeling of community and friendship with others in your life.

Chapter 2

Personal Sage and Smudge Rituals

As you search for ways to feel a greater connection to the flow of energy in your life, or seek to enhance your personal growth work on a spiritual and emotional level, one very powerful tool available to you is the Personal Sage and Smudge Ritual. In the following chapters you will find practical information about many ways of using Sage and other sacred smoke herbs to clear and heal your personal space. Some of the chapters offer a detailed procedure for carrying out specific Sage and Smudge rituals or ceremonies. And you will find stories of how people like yourself have created benefit and transformation in their lives with their personal Sage and Smudge ceremonies.

Many of these people had no experience with the process of performing a Sage and Smudge ritual the first time they tried one on their own. Although Sage and Smudge rituals or ceremonies are often learned through observation, explanation or "hands-on" teaching and learning opportunities, it may not be possible for every person to find someone who can guide them.

Some of you may have participated in a Sage and Smudge ritual or ceremony of some kind previous to attempting one on your own. A few of you may have heard about one from a friend or a teacher. Maybe you feel a desire to do spiritual work, and are searching for something more than meditation or study, contemplation or conversation to enhance your process. Performing Sage and Smudge rituals for personal clearing, healing and transformation work is one way to get in touch with how you balance the practical aspects and experiences in your life with the spiritual, intuitive and "curious", ever-searching aspects of your "real" (authentic) self.

Hands-on experience is the best teacher of how and when to carry out your own Sage and Smudge ceremonies, rituals and processes. And with the help of this guidebook and your own intuition, you will soon be able to experience the power and benefit of using Sage and other herbs to clear and to heal your personal space, and to expand your own sense of personal well-being and connection to the world you live in!

PERSONAL CLEARING, HEALING AND TRANSFORMATION WORK

Sage and Smudge can be used daily to clear and heal your personal space. Special rituals or ceremonies using Sage and Smudge - your personal "Spirit Smoke Rituals" - can celebrate and affirm positive changes as you experience them. They can help you explore your feelings about your world, and the people and things in it. As you explore various facets of your life using Sage and Smudge as your tool for personal growth, it might be a good idea to keep a personal journal of the things you observe or learn, and the specific rituals you carry out. A journal helps you to keep a record of your own experiences and feelings as they happen and you are able to refer back to your notes, thoughts and conclusions as you continue to work with Sage and Smudge in a personal way.

The best way to really become familiar with your "personal space" and prepare for a Personal Sage and Smudge Ritual or Ceremony is to focus on your intent, using all of your senses. Use this exercise to help you focus, to consider your personal responses to an object, a room, a person, an experience or a specific place or environment:

1. Take a good look at whatever (or whomever) you are considering, and really ***see*** what is there, see the reality you perceive with your physical eyes. Then close your eyes briefly, and concentrate on what you saw, remembering the details of it (or them). Explore with your mind what you "see" in your mind's eye when you think about the object, environment or person you are focusing on. (If you are considering someone who is not present, use a picture if you have one. Otherwise, visualize them in as much detail as you possibly can in your mind's eye. If you are considering a situation or an environment you want to transform - stay focused on the feelings that come to mind, try to create a "visual" image of the people or circumstances involved.)

2. Sit quietly and just listen to the sounds of your world in this moment, or think about the sounds you associate with the object of your focus. Think about any sounds that

disturb you. Think about how your world sounds when you are in a happy frame of mind. (This may be difficult, because we live in a world that surrounds us with sounds of all kinds almost every moment of the day. But you can begin to "listen" at times when things are going well, when you feel very frustrated, or when you feel happy, so that you will have sounds to think of in the future when you do this exercise.)

3. Does a scent come to mind? Is there a particular scent you like? One you don't like? Can you create an ambience around you that is pleasing to your senses? What would you need to do?

4. Touch, or imagine touching some part of that which is the focus of your attention. Imagine touching the object you are considering, or some part of the body of a person you are thinking of, or something in a room or an environment you are focusing on. Think about how it would feel to your fingers. How does it feel, on a purely physical level to touch it? to touch them?

5. Do you like the feeling you have when you are in this space, with this object, with a person, in the midst of an experience? Does it feel good to you? Close your eyes and really focus inward, on what you are feeling as you think about or visualize the object, the space, the person or the experience. Would you like

to feel more of what you are feeling? Or do you not like the feeling?

After you have considered your personal responses to a specific object, room, person, experience or environment, if you find that any aspect of your response is negative, consider creating a ceremony using Sage and Smudge to clear and heal this part of your reality. You may want to write down your initial thoughts or your answers to the above questions at this point, so you can compare these notes with ones you might write after you have carried out your personal Sage and Smudge ritual.

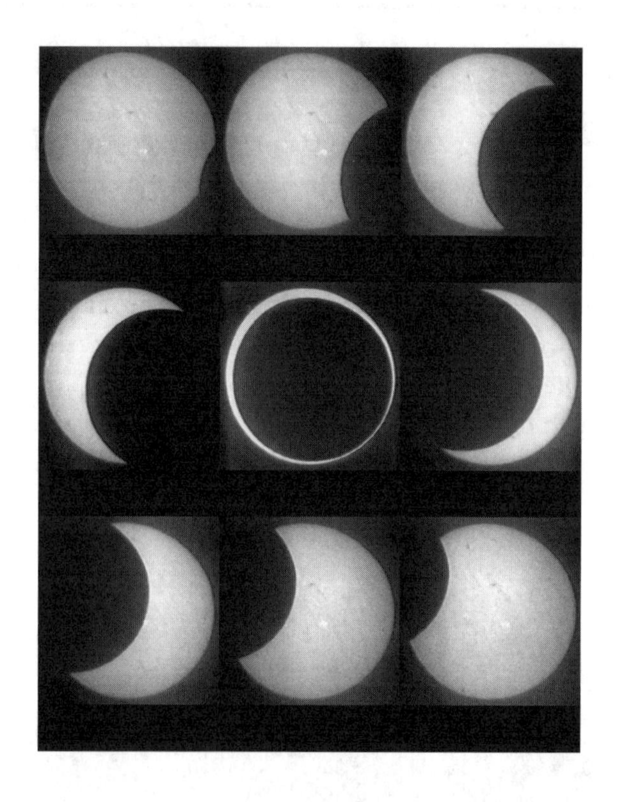

Chapter 3

When?

"Time is of the essence!"

Here are some examples of specific times you might want to perform personal Sage and Smudge rituals for best results. They are organized according to the phases of the Moon ("Moon Phases"), also sometimes called "Lunar Phases". You will find information about the phases of the

Moon in your local newspaper, in the "Farmer's Almanac", in an Astrological Planetary Guide, online and in many calendars. For the sake of simplification in this book, the cycle of the movement of the Moon during a Lunar Month is divided into "quarters", with each quarter representing approximately a week in time. You can carry out specific Sage and Smudge rituals on the day a Lunar Phase (or Moon Phase) begins - after the time indicated in your newspaper or calendar for when the phenomenon occurs. Or you can perform your ceremony or ritual during the week following the beginning of a particular Lunar Phase, until the beginning of the next one.

New Moon

Moving into a new home
Moving into a new apartment
Starting a new job
Starting a business
Starting a new project
Opening a Bank Account
Dating a new person
Buying a new car
Buying a new wardrobe
Having a make-over
Starting a diet
Starting a new health regime
Starting an exercise program
Arrival of a new pet
To celebrate the birth of a child
To celebrate the beginning of a New Year
To celebrate a birthday occurring during the month

These ceremonies are often fun. The New Moon is both an exciting and hope-filled time. Sage and Smudge rituals to celebrate them often reflect the positive nature of the event, how exciting it is to experience a "new beginning" in your life! It is good to express thankfulness and optimism as you carry out the ritual, also to mention (out loud) the things you envision that will bring you satisfaction and happiness as a result of the new experience.

First Quarter Moon

Re-decorating your home or apartment
Doing Feng Shui in your living or work space
Reconstruction or adding on to your home
Repairing or improving something
Expanding your area of expertise through study
Expanding your work responsibilities
Seeking a promotion
Expanding your customer base
Promotional activities
Increasing business
Increasing income (or seeking a raise)
Assuming more responsibility in a club or organization you belong to
Moving into a more intimate relationship with a partner
Improving your current relationships
Exploring investment opportunities
Actively participating in a cause
Taking action to change something in your personal life
Taking legal action against another party

These ceremonies can be quite intense! They are performed when you know there will be many challenges to face, and you feel willing to experience growth on many levels. A Sage and Smudge ceremony at the time of a First Quarter Moon time helps you focus on the challenges as you prepare to meet them over time. As a result of this type of ceremony, you become aware of opportunities for personal benefit all around you, and find ways (and the help you need) to achieve success in your endeavors.

The main focus of Sage and Smudge rituals during the First Quarter Moon is on a desired outcome. Think about what you want to achieve. It is good to express your vision and your expectations of a future outcome out loud as you do these rituals. Think about (and affirm out loud) what efforts you are willing to make or what you are willing to offer to achieve success, as you strive to reach your desired outcome, the goal you have in mind. Repeat these thoughts out loud as you perform your Sage and Smudge ritual or ceremony.

Full Moon

Selling a home
Selling a vehicle
Selling personal items you no longer need
Advertising for sales of all kinds
Offering your resignation
Ending a relationship
Filing Divorce Papers
Serving Divorce Papers
Leaving one home or area to move to another
Leaving home for college

Leaving home to start living on your own

Leaving school

Joining 12-step programs

Stopping smoking

Clearing clutter

Garage sale

Removing negative energies

Removing stressful situations and people from your life

Working to understand your anger and frustration about a specific situation

Preparing to give up bad habits of any kind

Full Moon Sage and Smudge ceremonies can take place when you desire an ending of some kind, and need someone else to help you achieve your goal. A Sage and Smudge ceremony at the Full Moon is performed to help you focus on things you would like to come to an end. You need to include an "invitation" to another to assist you, or help you achieve the ending you seek.

For instance, if you no longer want your car or your house, you need someone else to buy it. Or if you are ending your relationship, you need to communicate this to your partner. Their subsequent actions will affect your progress towards independence. If you are leaving home to attend college, you need the people in your family (and others in your life) to support your endeavor, and encourage your progress - and you need people at the college to welcome you and offer you a sense of continuity so that you will be able to accomplish your goals. Even if you are prepared to give up a bad habit, you need to find a good reason for doing so (which might mean that the opinions or wishes of other people are involved in your decision). It is helpful if you have a clear image of what new habit, behavior or routine is going to replace the old one!

A Full Moon Sage and Smudge ritual is a two-part or two-step process. You need to focus on what needs to "leave" your life, and then what you are going to replace it with. When an ending is desired and you are willing and prepared to take some action in the world to accomplish your goal, and you need someone (or something) else's participation to make it happen, then it is time for a Full Moon Sage and Smudge Ritual.

You may feel sad, empty, at a loss, or regretful about the ending which needs to take place, but you are prepared to take the necessary action on a personal level. On the other hand, you may feel thankful and relieved about an ending you have been working towards, or striving to attain, and grateful that others are helping you in your process. In any case, a Personal Sage and Smudge ceremony or ritual performed during the Full Moon phase is meant to indicate that a period of your life or a long-term situation is coming to a close. You are now ready to move on, and you are looking forward to having something new in your life!

The main focus of Sage and Smudge rituals at the Full Moon is often on "actively changing some aspect of your life". There is "the past" that has brought you to this place or decision, and "the future" you want, or want to create for yourself. In the best of cases, you are celebrating your accomplishments, the end of a positive, productive period of time in your life and looking forward to the future and the new opportunities. It is good to express your thoughts about the experience you are actively leaving behind out loud, to verbalize thankfulness/gratitude for the lessons you have learned from your experience, and to affirm the new energy, the new future or new experience you are seeking for your life.

Last Quarter Moon

Last payment on a credit card
Last payment on a vehicle
Last days at work, or at a specific job
Last days in your home before a move
Retirement
Children going off to college
Children moving out to live on their own
Letting go of pets
Clearing sleeplessness
Clearing your attachment to compulsive behaviors
Clearing space of negative influences
Clearing space (or objects) in general
Clearing stress
Letting go of anger and resentment
Asking for wisdom and understanding
Asking the Universe/Spirit for information
Asking for peace
Releasing karmic connections

Last Quarter Moon Sage and Smudge rituals, unlike the Full Moon Rituals, are about endings of all kinds that allow you to demonstrate your willingness, on a spiritual level, to "let go" . You may or may not be called upon to take any action outwardly in your world to achieve the outcome you desire (or to experience an outcome that is occurring at this time), other than performing a ritual to acknowledge and demonstrate your acceptance of where you are in your process and your life. And you don't need anyone else to be a part of the process at this point, all necessary action has already taken place, and now you simply want to express your spiritual awareness of completion (or "results") in some area of your life.

These ceremonies are often carried out when there is a need or a desire to release and let go of negative and hurtful experiences or behaviors, because they no longer serve a purpose in your life. However, in some instances, being able to let go of something can be a really positive and uplifting event - like paying off your vehicle, your student loan, your mortgage or a credit card - letting go of a debt! Also, many people have looked forward to retirement, or leaving a particular job for a long time.

In instances where some of the people involved in this ending are celebrating a new opportunity, and others are feeling a loss (like when children go off to college, or move out to live on their own, or when pets go to find new homes) both ends of the energy spectrum need to be acknowledged in your Sage and Smudge ceremony. Be very specific in your ritual, and recognize the importance of the experience from the perspective of all involved.

Other times

You may also want to create special Sage and Smudge ceremonies: to celebrate the birth of a new person, to celebrate someone's birthday, or to celebrate some other special event or anniversary. If you feel that you want to do a Sage and Smudge ritual, be creative as you plan for it. Choose a time when you are not under any pressure, wear colors and clothing you feel comfortable in, create a comfortable environment in which to carry out the ritual, and plan pleasant festivities or activities in conjunction with the ceremony.

Not all personal Sage and Smudge rituals require planning or special considerations. Some of them are very simple, take very little time, and can become good habits that help you to feel safe and protected in your life. For example, many people keep a small Sage wand just inside their front door and, as they enter their home at the end of the day, they quickly light the wand and smudge themselves for a minute or two to remove irritation, stress, unwelcome energy or influences they may have encountered during the day. The whole process may take only a few moments, but they feel relieved and have transitioned to being at home after having spent time in the world.

Chapter 4

Where?

Defining "Personal Space"

In addition to the variety of questions about when it might be a good idea to carry out a specific type of Personal Sage and Smudge ritual or ceremony, is the question of where to carry out such a process. To know the best places to perform your own personal sacred smoke rituals or ceremonies, you will need to define where you feel you exercise "personal power" in the world. Where do you feel safe? Where do you feel confident? Where do you interact with others who are important in your life? Where do you go when things are difficult? Where do you go to celebrate your successes (with or without others)? Where do you feel most secure, comfortable and relaxed and "at home" in your life?

Other factors impact your "personal space" and may include the people with whom you share your life experience - family members, lovers, friends, neighbors, co-workers and associates within your work environment. You might also want to include service providers, acquaintances or strangers (even pets) you meet or interact with in the course of your day. Whether you literally see them or not on a daily basis, whether you interact with them often or on a less regular basis - these people are "in" your personal space, and their energy vibrates around you and affects your life and your spirit on a more or less regular basis.

Additionally, when you think about things to include as you answer the question, "Who and what is in my personal space?", you may want to consider the furniture, objects, clothing and personal possessions you touch or use every day, whether these things belong to you, or to others. All of these people, places and things are part of your personal world, your environment. They are "in your personal space", and contribute their energy to your life.

Think about all of this as you consider where you might want to carry out a personal Sage and Smudge ritual. Some people feel very safe and comfortable in their bedroom, some in the office where they work. Others feel very dis-empowered at work or in their home environment. Some people enjoy driving, taking trips in a personal vehicle either on their own or with others. Some are very fearful of that type of activity, and nervous if they have to sit at the wheel for any amount of time in traffic. Some people prepare a special "altar" or area in their home that they use each time they perform a Personal Sage and Smudge ceremony. Some simply have a drawer where they keep the articles they need when they are going to use Sage and Smudge.

Here is an exercise that might help you to establish a definition of "personal space" that will work for you. You may want to have your journal handy as you work with these guidelines:

1. Prepare a list of all of the places where you spend time at home during a normal week. Include every area of your home: living room, dining room, bedroom, kitchen, bathroom, closet, garage, workshop, family room, etc.

2. Prepare a list of all of the places where you spend time away from home during a normal week. Include your vehicle, your job, and any other place you regularly go or spend time during the week.

3. Prepare a list of the people you interact with during the week or on a regular basis. These may be loved ones or friends you see often, or people you work with on a daily basis during the week. This list may also include people you talk with by phone, friends, family, co-workers or business associates and others who exchange email communications with you, and anyone else with whom you interact on a regular basis. During the minutes or hours you consciously devote your attention to them, but also when you are not consciously aware of them and they are simply "in the background" of your daily life, you are spending your time "with" these people! Their "essence" and personality are actually in your "personal space", whether or not they are actually in your presence or part of your conscious focus!

4. Now sit quietly with your first list, and think about the various areas of your home

where you spend time. Think about how you feel as you are spending time in the various areas. How do you feel when you get up in the morning? How do you feel when you are having breakfast or dinner? How do you feel when you are with other people in some part of your home and how do you feel when you are alone? How do you feel at night when you go to bed?

5. Sit quietly with the second list, and think about how you feel being in the various environments outside your home you spend time in during your week. How did you feel today? How did you feel last Tuesday?

6. Close your eyes and visualize the people you interact with on a regular basis, and think about how the relationship feels to you. Are you excited about spending time with the individuals on your list? Are you quiet when you are around them? Are you encouraged to be "who you are" when you spend time with them? Would you say you were in a good(?) or a challenging(?) relationship with the people on your list. Do you benefit from knowing and interacting with these people? Do they benefit from knowing you? Do you encourage them to be "who they are"? Do you benefit them, and do they appreciate you? Do they benefit you, and do you appreciate them?

7. Now make a list of the places that feel best to you, the people you most enjoy spending

> time with, and of the activities you are involved in that give you the most satisfaction. Also make a list of the places where you feel most uncomfortable, and the people or circumstances that make you the least comfortable.

As you sit afterwards with your lists and your own comments and thoughts, be aware that the places in your home that feel most comfortable to you are the ones you want to use when you do your own Personal Sage and Smudge rituals. Use them, for instance, for clearing and healing energy, objects, issues or relationships. For example, if you are very comfortable and happy in the kitchen, this might be an excellent place for you to carry out the type of Sage and Smudge ritual where you need to "clear" the energy field of an object that you associate with some form of negativity, negative feelings (and associations). And it might be just the place to perform a clearing and healing ritual for a challenging relationship!

If there are areas that are not so comfortable for you by comparison, then these may be areas that need your attention - areas where you need to carry out a clearing ceremony using Sage and Smudge to remove any negative energy from the space. You may want to focus on them first, and perform clearing and healing personal Sage and Smudge rituals in these spaces as soon as you can. You will find instructions on how to carry out specific types of Sage and Smudge rituals for a variety of rooms, spaces, objects, people, and issues as you read the following chapters.

In addition to carrying out specific clearings of this type, people commonly smudge their homes on a regular basis -

even for just a few moments at a time. Sometimes they simply spend a few minutes in each room after their normal housecleaning routines have been carried out. Many people burn Sage to clear the energy in a room where an argument or disagreement has occurred, or when sadness, fear or loss have been the topic of a conversation. Some people like to perform a brief Sage and Smudge ritual before going to bed every night to ensure that their dreams are undisturbed by negative energy or bad feelings left over from the day. As you become more familiar with how to use Sage and Smudge to benefit your life, your intuition will be your guide, and you will know the "when" and "where" that works for you!

Chapter 5

How?

Practical Tips for Using Sage and Smudge

"Purification" is a lovely (and very spiritual) word to use in the context of Personal Sage and Smudge rituals. It is the goal of the process you set in motion as you carry out a Sage and Smudge Clearing and Healing ritual of any kind. You want to be able to focus - concentrate - on your clearing, healing and purifying process during the ritual, without being distracted by practical considerations! You need to be able to focus on the outcome you want to achieve, to have a plan or an outline to follow, and know what you are going to do as you proceed and carry out the actual process of the ritual.

Start by selecting the herbs you want to use by thinking about the outcome you want to achieve. Then you need to decide when you are going to perform the ritual, where it will be carried out, which Sage and Smudge "tools" you are going to use with your herbs during the ritual to facilitate the process. There is a check list at the end of this chapter you can refer to as you organize and prepare to carry out your own personal Sage and Smudge rituals.

The preparation stage is important because you don't want to be distracted from your concentration and focus during the course of the rituals themselves. You want to be organized and know that you will be free to focus your energy on your intent, on the process itself and on your desired outcome.

As you carry out your Personal Sage and Smudge rituals and ceremonies you need to be able to let go of any worry that you are not "doing the ritual right" or that you might have "forgotten something important". You succeed best when you are able to be in the moment, experiencing your sacred smoke ritual as you create it.

One way to make sure that you can be "in the moment" as you are performing your ceremonies and rituals, is to have a clear idea of what you want to accomplish, which "tools" you will use to assist you in your clearing and healing work, and how you are going to do the ceremony itself. This chapter provides practical and useful tips and some general information about working with a variety of "tools" to create powerful Sage and Smudge rituals.

In following chapters you will find descriptions of a variety of personal Sage and Smudge rituals and ceremonies, and suggestions that will help you personalize them. In Chapter 1 you will find a list of the various herbs commonly used in Sage and Smudge work, and a summary of their special attributes. Chapter 3 offers a list of times people commonly carry out personal Sage and Smudge rituals or ceremonies. And, if you keep a personal Sage and Smudge journal, you will over time evolve your own list of when, where and how you do your own personal Sage and Smudge work.

Practical Tips

The easiest way to prepare to do a Personal Sage and Smudge Healing Ritual, is to follow many of the suggestions in this guidebook and to purchase your Sage and Smudge products and tools. You will find them in alternative bookstores, in health or natural food stores, and in gift shops specializing in metaphysical, herbal and self-help items. And you can order them directly from specialty herb growers, directly from American Indian suppliers, and others who advertise them on the Internet. (Note: It is a good idea to buy organic herbs whenever possible.)

Of course, you may want to grow Sage (and other herbs) in your garden, or collect Wild Sage yourself (in places where that is permitted). It is also possible that you don't have a garden, you can't collect the herbs anywhere near where you live, and you don't plan to travel to a place where the herbs grow in their natural environment, yet still you still want to grow your own herbs. In some areas Sage (and other herbs) can be cultivated on your patio in a flower box or flower pot! Some people even succeed in growing herbs in a flower pot on a window sill in their apartments!

The kind of Sage or other herbs you are able to grow depends a lot on your geographic location, the weather and type of soil you plant them in, and the care you are able to give them. If you plan to grow your own herbs, consult a local Nursery or Garden Store. Then, depending on the kind of Sage (and herbs) you grow, you may be able to make your own Sage and herb bundles, wands or sticks to use in the rituals you perform.

If you are going to use Sage and other herbs in their loose form in your rituals, dry the leaves, twigs, needles or blooms individually. Leaves, twigs, needles and blooms can be spread out on a piece of screen wire or netting, on a drying rack, or simply on paper towels on a cookie sheet. Then place them on a high shelf in a well-ventilated dark and dry place so they will be disturbed as little as possible by outside influences during the drying process. Turn the loose herbs weekly as they dry, so that they dry evenly. When they are completely dry, place each of the herb varieties separately in well sealed glass jars and keep them in a dark place until you are ready to use them. Bring the herbs you are going to use in personal Sage and Smudge ceremonies or rituals together (either whole or crushed) at the time you are ready to carry out your ritual.

If you would like to make your own herbal "wands" , "sticks" or "bundles" to use in Sage and Smudge rituals, start with fresh (or only slightly/partly dried) stalks and leaves or twigs of the herbs you have selected. Some suggest that the best time for this type of spiritual work is at the Full Moon while others recommend preparing herbal wands, sticks, bundles, sachets or pouches at the time of the New Moon. (You can find the time of the New Moon or the Full Moon in the newspaper, in the Farmers Almanac and in many calendars.) This is an example of where you can allow your intuition to guide you! (You will find suggestions for the appropriate time of the month to carry out the specific types of rituals themselves in Chapter 3.)

To create your own Sage and Smudge wands, sticks or bundles, start by selecting the herbs you want to include in your finished product. Arrange the stems, leaves, twigs, needles, etc., facing the same direction on a small towel, piece of felt or cloth. Place the colored string or embroidery floss you have chosen to bind your herbs together within easy reach. (See the section on "Color" in this chapter below for suggestions to help you choose an appropriate color of thread to use to bind your wands or sticks.) You can find the type of colored string or embroidery floss you need at craft and fabric stores.

Bring the base of the longest stems together in your less dominant hand as if you were going to hold them like a bouquet. Begin shaping and arranging the herbs that will be included in your wand as you gather the parts together. Wrap the colored string or embroidery floss you have chosen tightly around the base of the stems you are holding nine times, leaving a short two to three inch length of string as a loose end.

Continue to shape the wand by wrapping the string around the outside leaves of the wand you are creating, winding around, making nine loops from the base to the top of the wand (or stick) taking shape in your hands. (You want too bind the herbs quite tightly together.) It is suggested that you make nine loops as you bind upward, and nine as you loop back down the length of the Sage stick or wand, finally wrapping the base again nine times.

Tie off the end of your thread or embroidery floss tightly with the original loose string at the handle of your wand. Finally, cut off any tails of the string and place the newly formed Sage and Smudge wand or stick on a piece of screen wire or netting, on a drying rack, or simply on paper towels on a cookie sheet. Then they should be placed on a high shelf in a well-ventilated dark and dry place so they are disturbed as little as possible by outside influences during the drying process. Turn the wands or sticks weekly as they dry, so that they dry evenly.

Another alternative for the drying process is to use the loose ends of the string that remain after you have made a knot at the base of the wand to hang the smudge wand or stick upside-down in an elevated, cool (not cold), dry space until it becomes fully dried out. Make sure any Sage wand or stick is completely dry before using it in your rituals. (If necessary, re-wrap or re-bind carefully after the herbs are partly dry to ensure that you have a "tight" wand or stick to use in your rituals.)

The best place for drying herbs (in either a loose state, or in the form of a smudge wand or smudge stick), is in a cool, dark, well-ventilated area of your kitchen (such as a pantry), or some other area in your home that you select specifically for this purpose. The drying process may take a few days or weeks (for loose leaf or crushed herbs) to several months, depending on where you live, the usual weather conditions and humidity. Do not place herbs you intend to use in personal Sage and Smudge rituals and ceremonies in your oven to dry, even on a low heat setting. Allow the drying process to occur naturally. If you live in a very dry and sunny climate, the wands, sticks or bundles may be dried outdoors, as long as they are protected from the direct rays of the sun and from the wind. After the drying process is complete, always keep your Sage and Smudge tools dry when you are not using them, in a special drawer, or in a dark, cool place in your home.

If you have purchased a Sage and Smudge wand or stick and you find that you would like it wrapped with another type or color of string or thread, tie the thread or embroidery floss of your choice around the wand you have purchased in the manner described above, and then cut and carefully remove the original binding from the wand or stick. This can be done either at the time of the New Moon or the Full Moon. Or, you can add an additional wrapping of a color thread of your choice to an already formed and tied Sage and Smudge wand or stick. The most important thing to consider is that the "tool" that you are going to use for your personal Sage and Smudge ritual is as representative as possible of the purpose for which you intend to use it!

Tools

It is becoming increasingly popular to use Sage in the form of a wand or stick to carry out modern-day aromatic sacred smoke rituals to clear, heal and enhance a variety of personal environments, and to clear negative energy from our personal space. As we understand more about the role herbs played in ancient spiritual and religious prayer, devotion, ceremonies and rituals, we are discovering that we may have taken the essence of the sacred smoke herbs for granted.

Many of us may have simply derived benefit from the herbs by using them as culinary enhancements, or as a traditional resource in terms of alternative healing. But now, we can proactively bring the spiritual knowledge about these herbs into our lives as well, and share the excitement as we explore and discover the benefits of carrying out our own personal Sage and Smudge sacred smoke rituals.

Most of the time you can choose to use a simple Sage Wand, or loose leaves of Sage (especially White Sage) in your rituals. The dry, loose Sage leaves can be placed in a shell or in a heat resistant vessel you use especially for that purpose. There is no particular preference with regard to the form of Sage and Smudge product you choose to use for a Sage and Smudge ritual. You can choose from: Sage Stick, Sage Wand, Sage Bundle, a wand, stick or bundle including Sage and one or more other herbal smudge components, loose leaves, twigs, berries, needles or shavings (or even crushed herbs) in a ceramic, clay or metal vessel, a censer, a cauldron or a half-shell.

So, when you want to carry out a personal clearing or healing Sage and Smudge ritual, take your time and select the combination of herbs that make the best sense to you! And choose the form of the Sage and Smudge products that you feel most comfortable using. As you become familiar with the process of doing Personal Sage and Smudge rituals and ceremonies for various purposes, you will learn a great deal about how best to achieve the results you are seeking, and which types of herbs work well for you - on their own, or in combination with one another. You will also learn when to use a wand or a stick, and when it is more appropriate to use the loose form of the herbs.

Using Sage and Smudge Wands and Sticks

The easiest way to start out is to buy a Sage Wand or a Sage Stick, or one that includes Sage and one other of the herbs you particularly want to include in your initial rituals. As you grow in experience you can consider using various herbs singly or in combination. Then you can start to build a collection of wands and sticks with the herbs you need for a variety of rituals, or you can purchase the loose herbs you prefer, combine them and burn them in the vessel of your choice. Consider which of the herbs offer properties you need for your specific personal clearing and healing projects - your own "Spirit Smoke" rituals and ceremonies.

If you are using Sage and Smudge wands or sticks in your ritual, you will hold the wand in one hand (usually your dominant hand) while it is lit, and move around freely wherever you need to go. Always have a small, heat resistant

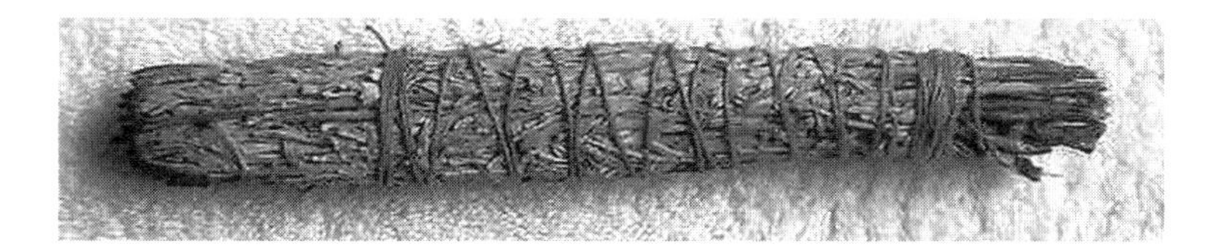

plate or bowl with you (that you can hold in your other hand) to catch any falling particles or ash from the wand as you move around a space freely during your ceremony or ritual, or as you move the wand around an unmoving object or person.

As you commence a Personal Sage and Smudge ritual, while you are carrying out the ritual, and at the end of it, say or read (out loud) the appropriate affirmations, prayers or words you have prepared. You can do this as you move with the wand around the space - or as you move the wand around yourself or any other person or thing you are clearing and healing with your ritual. You may want to write down the words on a parchment have your journal open to them, so you can say all you have in mind. (When you study the examples of personal Sage and Smudge rituals and ceremonies described in the following chapters, you will find suggestions for creating affirmations using clearing and healing words for your own ceremonies.)

If you use a Sage and Smudge wand or stick, it is quite common to use the same tool several times for a variety of purposes. You may not necessarily want your smudge wand

or stick to continue to be consumed by the heated embers burning within it after your ritual or ceremony has been completed. So, when you are done with your clearing and healing ritual, make sure that the fire (any embers burning in the wand) is completely extinguished.

The best way to do this is to dip the Sage and Smudge stick or wand top down in a bowl or glass of water briefly - submerging as much as you can of the wand. This method allows you to be completely sure that the wand no longer can continue to burn. Some people prefer not to use water to quench the fire, and they suggest tapping the smoking herb wand firmly in a bowl, and then holding the top of the wand against the bottom of the bowl until the smoke has died out. Others suggest putting the wand, top down, into a bowl or container filled with sand - which will extinguish any embers that may still be burning inside the wand.

Any method you use to extinguish the wand, check to make sure that it is cool to the touch, that no smoke of any kind is still rising from it after 10-15 minutes. Look carefully into the top of the wand, and hold the top of it in your hand to see if it feels cool to the touch. And then, for the sake of safety, place the wand or stick in the kitchen sink, laundry room sink, or even the bathroom sink or tub for a few hours - just to make positively sure any fire is completely "out" before you put it away. Keep your wands and sticks in the place you keep other Sage and Smudge ritual tools when you are not using them!

Using Loose Sage and Other Herbs

If you are going to select from an assortment of "loose" herbs, you will need several additional "tools" in order to create aromatic sacred smoke. One traditional method is to use a half shell as the vessel to hold the herbs you have selected to burn. And one of the most popular shells to use is the abalone shell. (These shells and other fire-resistant vessels will most likely be found where you buy Sage and other herbal items for the purpose of smudging to clear and heal personal environments.)

While some of the American Indian Shamans prefer not to use a shell, and choose other man-made, fire-resistant vessels to use in their ceremonies, those who do prefer the shell believe that using it brings in a balance of the elements -

Earth, Air, Fire and Water - to a ritual. (The element of Fire is represented because the herbs are lit and smoldering. The aromatic smoke itself represents the Air element. The herbs, having grown from the earth, represent the Earth element. And the shell represents the Water element.)

You may, instead of a half shell, choose to use a fireproof bowl, plate, ceramic pot, small baking dish, censer, brazier, or other vessel in which to burn your loose or crushed herbs, and you can, of course, place the dried herbs on burning logs in your fireplace. If you would like to try that, place the loose herbs on a piece of wood that is glowing (not flaming), and the scent of the burning herbs will enhance the aroma of the smoke from the fire, and create a healing energy in the room.

As you commence a Personal Sage and Smudge ritual, while you are carrying out the ritual, and at the end of it, say or read (out loud) the appropriate affirmations, prayers or words you have prepared. You can do this as concentrate on the burning herbs - or as you move around the room clearing and healing energy with your ritual. You may want

to write down the words on a parchment have your journal open to them, so you can say all you have in mind. (When you study the examples of personal Sage and Smudge rituals and ceremonies described in the following chapters, you will find suggestions for creating affirmations using clearing and healing words for your own ceremonies.)

While it is possible to "light" loose herbs and crushed or ground herbs directly with a match, small lighted stick or cigarette lighter, you may want to maintain a more consistent heat/smudge level during your Sage and Smudge rituals. Then you will need a source of heat that remains steady for some time - especially during longer Sage and Smudge rituals and ceremonies.

In the types of stores that sell incense and herbs (or from other suppliers of Sage and Smudge herbs), you will be able to find small, usually round, packages of a special kind of charcoal "brick" made to use with powdered incense, or in Sage and Smudge rituals. These special charcoal bricks are usually round, and come wrapped in "foil", and you remove the individual bricks from their packaging and burn them one by one as needed during the course of your sacred smoke ritual or ceremony. This type of charcoal brick is prepared differently than the ones you would buy for your outdoor grill and has not been treated with any chemicals that would interfere with the natural qualities of the herbs you are planning to burn in your rituals.

To use this Sage and Smudge method, place a charcoal brick in the vessel you want to use for the ritual, and light it when you are ready to start. When lit, the small charcoal bricks start burning easily and remain hot for quite some time - so that when you sprinkle or place your loose or crushed herbs on the charcoal brick, the herbs will start to burn, keep burning and creating smudge for your ritual for some time. During most rituals you will probably need to add more of your herbs on top of the charcoal brick from time to time, if you notice that the amount of smoke is lessening.

When you use loose or crushed Sage leaves (and other herbs) in your rituals and ceremonies, the smudge holder can be placed in the center of the room, or in the area you have determined to use for your ritual. The bottom of the container will become very hot, so be sure that you will not need to move it until the ritual is completed and the pot/container has cooled. You may want to have a special heat-resistant flat stone or other protective material to place under the container to protect your floor or the furniture on which you set the smudge holder during your Sage and Smudge rituals.

You sometimes will want to carry the holder in one hand in order to be able to move around during your personal Sage and Smudge ritual. You will need a hotpad, or other protective gear to wear on the hand that "carries" the holder with the smoldering smudge during the ritual. In your other hand, you can carry the "tool" you plan to use to help you move the smoke around the object or space you are clearing. While it is possible to move the smoke with the motion of your hands, or with your breath, it is more common to use a feather or a fan to help you do this.

At the beginning of your ritual as the smoke first rises from the herbs in your vessel, encourage it to move upward, and then in the four directions, North, East, South and West as you commence your clearing ritual, and then out

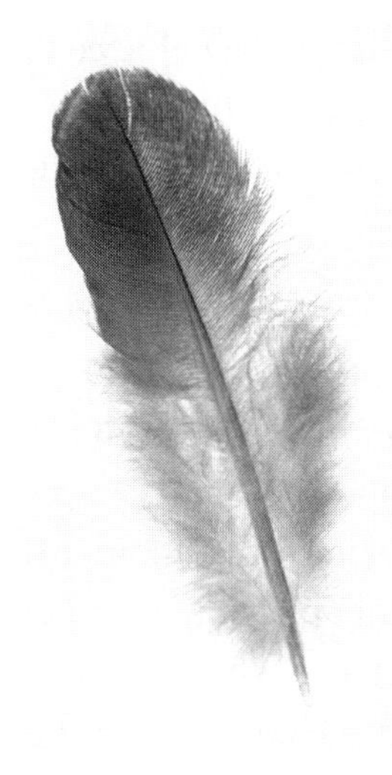

and around with very short, quick motions using either the feather or the fan. While this is being done, it is appropriate to read, chant or say your ceremonial "clearing and healing words".

When you complete a sacred smoke ceremony in which you have used loose Sage leaves or any combination of loose herbs, simply allow the herbs to continue to smoke and burn until they "burn out" on their own.

Lighting Sage and Smudge

Before you do your first ritual with loose herbs, check to see whether you have a smoke detector in the space where you plan to carry out your work. If you do, you may want to check the ventilation in the room or space, and have a window at least slightly open to let out some of the smoke as you carry out the process. It is very disturbing to have the alarm go off and interrupt your work in the midst of your ceremony.

The final tool that is necessary for this process - whether you are using a wand, stick, bundle or loose herbs - is something you can use to ignite the Sage and Smudge for the ritual. If you are using the loose Sage leaves or other loose herbs in a heat-resistant vessel, one way to proceed is to place a small brick of charcoal in the bottom of the vessel and light it. Allow the charcoal to become very hot. When the charcoal is hot you can place your Sage leaves (or crushed Sage and other herbs) on top of the charcoal. The heat from the charcoal brick will cause the herbs to burn, and smoke will rise indicating you can begin your clearing ritual.

You can also place a small number Sage and other dried leaves (or a small amount of crushed Sage leaves, twigs and other herbs) directly in the bottom of your container. Strike a match (preferably a wooden one at least a couple of inches in length) and allow it to burn for just a moment. When you see that the match is burning, place it carefully on the herbs in the container. If there is a very small amount of smoke, blow very gently to encourage the flame to spread to more of the herbs. If there is a considerable flame, gently blow out the fire from a careful distance, and leave the herbs smoldering inside the bowl, adding more herbs as you need to keep a steady smudge rising during your ceremony. You may need to use several matches to get started, or to light additional amounts of the smudge herbs during a longer clearing, so keep the matches accessible!

If you are using a Sage and Smudge Wand/Stick, the easiest way to light it is to hold the wand in one hand, flick on a cigarette lighter or a "fireplace lighter" with the other hand and hold the light to the top end of the wand until the wand starts burning. You can use matches, but it will usually take several attempts before you can start a good fire in your wand. So you will definitely want the kind of match that burns more than a few seconds before it singes your fingers! You might want to try using the foot-long wooden matches usually used for starting a fire in a fireplace - as they will burn long enough to light the Sage Wand or Sage and Smudge Stick. Or you can light a dried twig or a thin piece of wood, and use that as a "match" to help you ignite the Sage wand itself.

Usually there will be a flame as the lighter touches and sets fire to the dried herbs in the wand or stick. When you see that the Sage is ignited, gently blow out the flames and see if the wand/stick continues to smoke. If it does not, repeat this procedure, until you see a steady amount of smoke rising from the wand. You will want to carry the lighter with you if you are in motion during the clearing ceremony, because it is possible that you may have to re-light the wand or stick several times before it is hot enough to continue smudging on its own. (Remember, it is a good idea to have a fireproof bowl, shell or plate with you, holding it under the wand as you go, in case little bits of the herbs or embers fall while still smoldering hot or as ash.)

It is quite common to use a Sage and Smudge wand or stick several times for a variety of purposes. You do not necessarily want your smudge wand or stick to be consumed by the fire after your ritual or ceremony has been completed. So, when you are done with your clearing and healing ritual, make sure that the fire (and any embers burning in the wand) is completely extinguished. See above for more details.

Color Choices

Now that you know the types of Sage and Smudge tools you need, and which ones you will want to buy or create for yourself, let's take a look at the significance of the color choices you can make. For instance, Sage wands and sticks are wrapped with thread or embroidery floss. The color of the thread or floss is meant as an enhancement to the energy which spreads with the sacred smoke during the ceremony or ritual you are performing. If you use loose Sage leaves or a combination of herbs to smudge, you will burn them in a vessel intended for that purpose. Choose the "color" of your vessel carefully.

Special "Spirit Smoke" rituals or ceremonies using Sage and Smudge help focus your intent on healing and clearing difficulties or challenges in your life. And Sage and Smudge ceremonies can celebrate and affirm positive changes as you experience them.

So, whether you are buying a tool that has already been made, or you are selecting thread or floss to bind your own wand or stick, or a vessel in which to burn your loose herbs, color will become a significant part of your smudge ceremony or ritual. By choosing your colors carefully, you can achieve very powerful results!

Many times intuition "pulls" or attracts you to pick up a certain wand, stick or vessel to use in your ceremonies or rituals. It's almost as if you know, on a subconscious level, what energy or effect is the right one for you at that time. It can be interesting to turn to the information here on color, and find out which type of "energy" you were feeling was necessary in your life or to your purpose when you selected the item you chose. What was it that felt so "compelling" to you in some way at the time of your purchase? Let's apply what we know about color and how it is used in our world, to understand why we choose (or might think about choosing) the colors we include in our Sage and Smudge rituals and ceremonies.

Primary Colors

The "Primary Colors" are red, blue and yellow. These three cannot be created by mixing any other colors. When there is a primary, really strong need for results from your smudging, choose one of these colors to add strength to your desired purpose.

Shades of color are created by combining black or white with the color to either heighten or darken the color energy. Tones and nuances of color often occur when colors from at least two of the three "color families" are blended together. Additional colors of the scale occur when shades and tones are combined. These create the kaleidoscope of color impressions and awareness which speak to our subconscious mind, communicating their various messages in ways we will now attempt to understand on a more conscious level.

The Red Family

The color red is the maximum attention-grabber. It represents a very primal energy often present in a new cycle, in the excitement of meeting someone new or launching an activity. Two words strongly associated with red are "Desire" and "Will". Opportunities, possible sudden change, movement, vitality and denial of restrictions are energies represented by red.

When we see someone whose face is "red" we often associate with the more negative aspects of the color: anger, pain, frustration, embarrassment, etc. Red engenders strength, courage, anger, enthusiasm and can be used to reduce depression, fear and worry. It is often used to suggest warmth, passion, virility, life, power and bravery.

Crimson to Pink: Various shades of red are created by blending red and white, or red and black. These shades make up the members of "The Red Family". Red and white provide the pastel shades of the palate, from rose to pink. Pastel Pink is particularly good for hiding strength, reducing ambition and relieving stress. Mixing black and red leads to the darker statements of red - from a dusky red to shades of crimson.

The Blue Family

The color blue expresses the energy of a labor or a journey of the mind, a process where considered thought is a part of any result. The effect of blue is to slow down any unfocused direction of energy. Blue brings you a vision or perception of the issues and areas of your life that are out of balance, and encourages you to work towards viable solutions. Although blue has many positive attributes it can, under certain circumstances, indicate a lack of feeling, i.e. coldness or withdrawal; sometimes sadness or distance (we sing "the Blues"), or something that might happen "once in a Blue Moon".

Blue energy aids in spiritual healing, meditation, development of the higher mind, peace, beauty and the harmony of the creative process. Truth, poise and serenity are accessed with this color. Blue energy combats feverish conditions, irritation and frustration. Accessing the power of blue clears the way for the consciousness of your will to supply all that is needed to satisfy your soul's need for personal growth.

Cobalt to Sky Blue: The members of "The Blue Family" are called forth by mixing blue with white, or blue with black. The colors we may most often think of are Royal Blue, Cobalt Blue, Navy Blue or Steel Blue (black, white and blue combinations). These and other members of "The Blue Family" represent the various types of enlightenment the journey of mind over matter can bring into personal experience. Concentration and mental focus are aided by these colors.

The Yellow Family

Yellow is the color connected with the power of the Sun (solar power) and the energy provided by the Sun to Earth - the energy that allows life to exist in all its forms on Earth (solar energy). It brings a feeling of sunlight and flowers, and makes things look large, exciting and cheerful. Since ancient times, this color has been associated with one of the vital organs, the liver.

The color yellow represents the energy of synthesis, expressing growth through experience, and aspirations for respect and recognition. It also is associate with "memory" - the past that has helped us become who we are now, and it urges us "to remember" what is important to us as we move into the future. On a negative note, yellow is a connotation for someone who is fearful, cowardly or weak ("Everyone knows he's a yellow-belly!") We describe certain kinds of publishing as "yellow journalism". And the yellow coloring that comes with age (something or someone who is old) may be perceived as a sign of physical weakness or fragility, or poor health.

However, yellow is the color best used to stimulate the mental faculties. It stimulates the creation of new thoughts and ideas, and the process of visualization. It symbolizes history (the "yellowed" pages of time) and supports the process of memory. Yellow arouses optimism, cheerfulness and understanding; it engenders clarity and awareness. Yellow has a high attention value (i.e. legal pads, or MacDonald's Golden Arches). It also encourages youth, optimism and a sunny outlook on life.

Gold and **Sunshine** are members of "The Yellow Family". The powerful beauty of gold, the metal which reflects this color, has made it one of the most desirable of all things on earth.

When Color "Families" Combine

Orange: This color derives from a combination of red and yellow. Although not popular as clothing in Western cultures, it is a color with very positive connotations. Orange is energizing and has a high attention value (prisoners in their bright, orange jumpsuits definitely stand out!). Orange indicates health and vitality. It represents enlightenment, abundance, prosperity, middle life and harvest time.

"The Orange Family" includes bright to pastel, everything from fire engine red, to peach (red, white and yellow), salmon, sunrise shades, the shifting shades of sunset (add some black to the mix) and many popular "Southwestern" tones.

Purple: A mixture of red and blue, purple brings together the subliminal strengths and weaknesses of both of these colors and calls out to the best (represented in the robes of Kings, Priests, the wealthy and the highest authorities in the various branches of knowledge and hidden wisdom) and the worst (extravagance, greed, ego and manipulation) within the human soul.

Originally the color purple was pressed from the shells of tiny sea creatures and distributed by the Phoenicians; it was more costly (in money and lives) than gold, and could only be afforded or worn by the upper classes of the time, as international law regulated its sale. Throughout the Middle Ages and into our time, purple has been worn as an expression of power and has attracted its antitheses, weakness.

Lavender to Maroon: These shades of "The Purple Family" are developed by mixing with black, to create the rich nuances of maroon. Red and blue can be blended with white to create the softer hues of violet and lavender.

Green: Mixing blue and yellow in various proportions results in "The Green Family" palate. This is the color scale which makes our Earth so beautiful. Even from space our planet can be identified by the richness of these tones, appearing almost like a giant emerald or turquoise to the observant eye.

Green, with its connotations of growing life, richness and abundance, often symbolizes wellness and the healing energy that is required to achieve this state (many hospitals and health care facilities use shades of green in their décor). Green can also represent a need for healing on many levels - physically, mentally, psychologically and spiritually.

Green is symbolic of safety (green light = GO), youth, nature, expansion (growth), and may be indicative of instances where caution is necessary (i.e. mold is green, and "envy" has been assigned the color green in many languages.)

Brown: The combination of all three of the primary colors gives us this color. Earthy, "grounded", responsible, reliable, trustworthy, plentiful - many such words describe the energy of brown and "The Brown Family", from beige to rust in color. I am sure we all can remember a pair of brown shoes which just "never wore out"; or observed the beige/brown uniforms of local sheriffs' departments, the khaki of the military uniforms, etc.

We have come to associate nuances of brown without necessarily noticing the individual qualities of "brownness". It is indeed a background, yet necessary, color in our lives.

Black is technically an absence of color. Blackness brings to mind nighttime, caves, dark places - creating in some people a sense of safety, and in others a sense of mystery or fear. (And whenever there is a mystery about something, there is a powerful urge to discover "the secret"!) The sense of being able to keep secrets, or of knowing more than is being revealed leads to a sense of power - the powerful energy of the essence of black.

White is the "color" which occurs naturally through the combination of all of the colors of a rainbow into a single focus. If you take a spectrum and place it in the light of the sun, all of the colors will be separated out, and you will be able to see the rainbow of colors that come together to create white. The essence of the energy of white is: light, clarity, openness, conscience and awareness.

Gray: With its energetic essence composed of a blend of black and white, gray clearly expresses the "in-between" qualities of both. All of the colors we perceive consist of some element of gray. Shades - dark or light - help communicate the shadowy language of color which shapes our lives. Use gray when you are thinking of the many nuances of experience and are seeking clarity or balance.

Silver: Luminescent gray (black and white). Use strands of silver or silver vessels to attract experience and benefit to any situation.

Checklist for Sage and Smudge Rituals

This is a checklist of practical "tips" to keep in mind as you incorporate the practice of Sage and Smudge rituals and ceremonies into your life:

¤ Keep your sage and smudge tools dry when you are not using them, in a special drawer, or a dark, cool place in your home.

¤ Keep lighters or matches out of the reach of children who might want to imitate what they have seen you do, unless you are supervising.

¤ Thoroughly prepare yourself before beginning any ritual. Know the reason, the process and the expected outcome before you start.

¤ Assemble all of your "tools" before you start a Sage and Smudge ritual or ceremony. Make sure you have enough time to carry out your sacred smoke work without interruptions.

If you are using a holder with loose Sage leaves, or crushed Sage and other herbs in your Sage and Smudge ritual, make sure you are using them in a fire-safe way. Remember, herbs can "pop"/"crackle"/"spark" on occasion, and may "jump" out of the container you have them in- possibly causing damage to a carpet or to your furnishings. Light and carry these loose herbs in holders meant for the purpose (such as a censer, ceramic bowl or a shell).

If you are using a censer, cauldron, shell, clay, ceramic or other heat-resistant container for your smudging rituals, and you are using loose Sage leaves, crushed Sage and other herbs or an herb "bundle" - with or without the special charcoal bricks recommended for the process - remember that your vessel will become very hot during the ritual. Know in advance where you will put your vessel down, if you are planning to carry it around!

If the sacred smoke ritual will be assigned a place in the room at the beginning of the ceremony and left there, select a safe spot to place your heat-resistent vessel in the room (or in your fireplace) before you start your ceremony. (Many people use a granite cutting board, one of the heat-resistant bricks or tiles that can be used for baking pizza in the oven, or a really good, thick pad made of some other kind of heat-absorbent material.)

If you are using a Sage and Smudge wand or stick make sure you are using this tool in a fire-safe way. Remember to carry a bowl, plate or shell with you as you move around the designated space for the ritual with a lighted smudge wand or smudge stick. Use it catch any ash that may fall during the smudging process.

Have a bowl with water or a container with sand nearby that you can use to extinguish the smoldering Sage Wand or Sage Stick when your Sacred Smoke ritual or ceremony is completed.

Never leave ritual or ceremonial Sage and Smudge burning in another room to go and answer the phone, or the door - or for any other reason. If you need to leave your ritual part-way through, extinguish all burning/smudging materials with water or sand, making sure no smoke (or heat) remains unattended.

Make sure that all wands and containers are cool to the touch (and dried out, if water was used to extinguish any embers, glow or heat before putting your Sacred Smoke tools away after using them for Sage and Smudge rituals and ceremonies.

***Note:* The smudge smoke from your rituals will permeate the air (and all objects and materials) in the space where you are carrying out your ceremony. You will want to be able to open a door or window to allow excess smoke to escape. This means you might not be able to carry out a Sacred Smoke ritual in a place where the windows cannot be opened, or where a shared air circulation system is part of a larger apartment or condominium complex or office environment.**

Chapter 6

Unable to Smudge?

In some instances it may be difficult or impossible for you to smudge, to light your Sage and other herbs to create aromatic smoke to clear and heal your space. This is a problem you might have if you live or work in a building with a central air heating and cooling system - and with windows you cannot open to "air out" your personal space. The sacred smoke from your ritual is, in this type of situation, carried into other apartments or offices via the interconnected air ducts!

The smoke and the scent of your personal sacred smoke rituals and ceremonies may cause problems for others who live or work in the same building when it reaches their personal space. You may also have family members or others sharing your personal space who are unwilling or unable (for physical/health-related reasons, for instance) to accept or allow Sage and Smudge rituals and ceremonies in the shared environment.

There are people who like the spiritual practice of smudging with Sage and other herbs, but who don't like the fact that the smoke penetrates their clothing, hair and furnishings (carpets, drapes, bedding, etc.). They are uncomfortable with the scent of the Sage and other herbs lasting for quite some time. In instances like this, it is difficult to explain to these people that the aromatic smoke from the Sage and other herbs was created with an intent to protect, heal and clear the environment - and the people in it. And that the lingering scent in the clothing and furnishings is a positive indication of the power of the herbs, and their ability to do what they are meant to do!

However, if you are someone who finds yourself in one of the above-mentioned situations, there are solutions to this conundrum. People have always used dried herbs and herbal extracts in a variety of ways to improve their health, their homes and personal environment and as part of their spiritual practices. No matter how people use them, the herbs themselves have always provided the benefit of their "clearing" and "healing" properties - their energy, so to speak.

If you would like to access the essence and power of Sage and the other sacred smoke herbs in your life, yet you do not want to (or cannot) smudge or burn these herbs, there are alternatives that might work for you. First of all, Sage and herbs of all kinds have been used down through the ages as "scent" or as essences in "perfume". These days it is quite common to find many sweet and pleasant herbs in potpourri, in sachets, in bath oils, cosmetics, body lotions, hand lotions, skin creams and potions of all kinds.

You probably have many of the herbs mentioned in Chapter 1 in your home already - perhaps in their culinary form, as part of your décor (as part of a wreath you might hang on your door at the holidays or as part of a bouquet of flowers in a vase or in a special decorative centerpiece you place on your dinner table). You probably also enjoy the scent of the herbs in the form of "Potpourri" or "sachets", scented candles and oils, or in the aromatherapy essences you prefer.

Potpourri is probably the most popular and easiest way to bring the benefit of dried sacred smoke herbs into your personal space to enjoy as part of your every-day life. Another way is to buy or make small sachets or pouches filled with your favorite herbs to place in enclosed storage areas. Potpourri and herbal sachets can be purchased at most department stores, drugstores, and at bed and bath stores all over the country. They may also be purchased from a variety of specialty stores, craft stores, health and whole food stores, and of course, from wholesale and retail outlets who market herbal products on the Internet.

Some people like to place small sachets filled with Lavender, for instance, in their dresser drawers or inside a pillow they will sleep on. Some place small, sweet-smelling sachets of mixed herbs or chips of cedar in among their woolen outerwear (sweaters and other warm winter garments) in clothing bags, or other storage areas. Some people keep their woolens in cedar chests, or place cedar chips or balls in their drawers or storage areas for a variety of reasons.

You will also find many of the herbs in this book listed as components in a variety of teas or tablets used or recommended by Alternative Health Professionals, especially practitioners in the fields of herbology, homeopathy, acupuncture, massage, etc. You can ask for advice from these professionals and others who know a great deal about the use of herbs, and find literature about the various herbs at health food stores and outlets. Or, you can find a great deal of information online about how to include herbs in your diet to enhance health and wellness. All of this, however, is not within the scope of this book.

The herbs we talk about in this book are in many recipes for foods we commonly eat, either as a spice or seasoning, or as a condiment served with a meal. Sometimes we, as consumers, find edible flower petals and various leaves and buds from plants commonly used in Sage and Smudge rituals in our salads, or our salad dressings. It is quite possible to select some herbs for their spiritual quality and include them in your diet, your choice of cosmetics and/or to include them in your life in some other way.

You might like to make your own "herbal essence oils" to use in culinary endeavors. One example of this is to place loose leaves of Sage in an attractive glass jar or bottle, pour over your favorite unflavored oil to within an inch or so of the top. Seal the bottle tightly, and allow it to stand in a cool place for at least 24 hours to a week before using your own "Herbal Essence Oil" to enhance the flavor of your food. When the flavor of the Sage, for instance, has enhanced the oil, you can then use your own "Sage Oil" in marinades, salad dressings or to fry your favorite foods (or drizzle on cooked foods before serving them). You can also use the dried (or fresh, whole) herbs of your choice by chopping, grinding or crushing them with a mortar and pestle before including them in your favorite recipes.

Perhaps you simply would like to grow fresh Sage and Smudge herbs in your home, or hang wreaths made with

dried twigs and leaves of the herbs in your kitchen or dining room.

You might like to include parts of the plants in decorative flower arrangements elsewhere in your home. It is not uncommon to see a wreath of Sage in the kitchen, dining room or pantry - certainly in homes everywhere, but even in fine restaurants! And Juniper can be a lovely addition to a holiday wreath hanging either outside the front door, in the family room in winter, winding up the railing of a staircase - or as part of a table decoration for a special celebration.

Casting

Many spiritual traditions have a practice called "casting" where herbs (and incense) are scattered in a space - much like flower girls strew flower petals in front of a bride as she walks down the aisle to meet her partner in front of the altar. If you personally like the smell of the various herbs, but cannot (for whatever reason) burn them to create sacred smoke, you can crush or grind dried herbs and use them in a "Casting" ritual or ceremony. You can sprinkle the crushed or powdered herbs in areas of your home you feel you would like to clear and heal - as you carry out your spirit work in much the same way you would do if you were going do a sacred smoke ritual or ceremony.

You might like to follow the example of others who, using a type of "Casting Ritual", sprinkle crushed or ground herbs from a salt shaker onto the doorstep or entrance-way to their personal space, or their home. When you or some other person enters your personal space across the area where the herbs have been "cast", you and they are cleansed of any stressful influences encountered out in the world prior to entering into your personal space. You might also like to sprinkle crushed herbs in your personal space after guests leave, to clear the energy within your home.

Some American Indian tribal rituals include "casting" cornmeal as part of a ceremony. They "cast" it either to the winds, or towards the heavens and then to the four corners of the earth (North, South, East and West). This ritual is meant to bring bounty, benefit and wealth to all who participate in the ceremony. You might like to combine cornmeal with Sage and other crushed herbs, and create your own "Wealth Ritual"!

You can plan to use Sage and other sacred smoke herbs in your own "Casting" ritual or ceremony for the purpose of clearing and healing your personal space and for enhancing and improving your life on a spiritual level. Use the times of the Lunar Phases (or Moon Phases) listed in Chapter 3 and other times mentioned elsewhere in this book as well as the Sage and Smudge ritual or ceremonial outlines in the following chapters as a guide to creating your own "Casting" rituals. Simply use the sacred smoke herbs in their crushed or ground form - without burning them.

If you would like to carry out complete "Casting Ceremonies" on your own, a more spiritual process would be to include the grinding or crushing of the herbs (by hand, in a mortar with a pestle) as part of your personal clearing and healing ceremony. You might chant the words of your ceremonial affirmations as you crush and grind the herbs, as well as when you "cast" them. In this way you will know that the essence of the herbs is fresh and new, and they have been handled in accordance with your purpose and intent.

All sacred rituals, all spiritual ceremonies offer you an opportunity to commune with your God, your Guides, your Guardians, your Angels - the positive energy that exists in your Universe. The form your ritual takes - whether you can perform a ceremony with sacred smoke, or whether your personal clearing and healing rituals and ceremonies are based on ceremonial "casting" - is less important than your intent as you use the herbs. In either case, use the time you devote to this spiritual work as an opportunity to be open and honest with yourself about your life. Focus on your own spiritual intent and growth, your own needs, wants and feelings and carry out your own personal rituals and ceremonies confident of a positive outcome!

The most important part of any ritual is that it allows a space in time for you to be in touch with the part of you that is everlasting, spiritual, and part of the greater Whole. Rituals and spiritual ceremonies are designed to clear your mind, body and spirit of any contaminating factors or thoughts that could cause harm to you or any other being. They serve to help you focus your consciousness inward, to separate your "self" from the mundane concerns of your every-day life, and to explore the creative and wonderful spirit within you.

Chapter 7

Clearing Your Bedroom

The White Sage Wand she is holding is about eight inches long and almost two inches around at its thickest point. The wand is tightly wrapped at the base with brightly colored thread. The thread has been wound in a pattern that continues up and around the sage twigs and leaves the length of the wand and almost to the tip of it, and has helped to bind the sage leaves firmly in place as they dried.

She holds that brightly bound base of her wand now firmly in her left hand as she lights the top of it with her lighter and watches the flames burn hungrily for a few moments as they ignite the dried White Sage. Then the flames become an even glow, as the Sage Wand and she become ready to do the clearing work. Smoke rises from the wand into the air with every move she makes, dancing as smudge will do with the movement of the air in the doorway where she is standing.

Placing the lighter in the pocket of her vest, she picks up the small ceramic bowl from the hall table outside her bedroom door. She will it use to catch any ash that might fall from the wand during the process of her clearing ritual. She glances quickly around to check that the matching ceramic pot with sand is in place outside the entrance doorway to the room. Now she turns her attention to the clearing and healing ceremony she is about to commence.

Standing in the doorway, she observes the smoke waft slightly to the left, and begins moving in the same direction the smoke indicated. As she moves into the room, she clearly states the purpose for her ceremony, "Cleanse and clear any negative energy from this bedroom." As she approaches the chest of drawers along the first wall, she notices that the smoke from her wand slows briefly, and sinks towards the floor.

She stops there and re-lights her wand, blowing gently on the flame to make sure that it turns into a glowing ember within the wand itself. Then as the smoke once again rises, she moved the wand gently from side to side, up and down along the front and sides of the chest, until the smoke clearly starts rising up towards the ceiling once again.

She faces the front of the chest and says out loud, "Clear and heal the energy surrounding this chest of drawers, the contents and anything placed on top of it of any negativity. Heal the energy of all items in and on this chest." She circles round the chest of drawers and continues to the first corner of the room. There she faces out into the room, holding the wand at the level of her heart, and repeats the purpose for her ceremony as an affirmation, "Cleanse and clear any negative energy from this bedroom." Then she continues along the next wall to a window that overlooks her back yard.

At the window, she carefully moves the Sage Wand along all of the edges of the window, careful not to touch the draperies and the shade with her lighted wand, and says, "Protect and guard this room from any intrusion of any kind, person or energy. Keep all negativity away from this bedroom."

Then she continues on to the next corner, moving the smoldering wand slowly around the cedar chest, saying, "Clear and heal the energy surrounding this cedar chest, and the contents within." She stops for a moment, checking to make sure that the sacred smoke rises upwards into the air before moving along the remaining length of the wall to the second corner of the bedroom. At the second corner she once again faces the center of the room and repeats her affirmations for the room, "Cleanse and clear any negative energy from this bedroom."

She continues her ritual, turning her attention to the open closet door, and moves her wand carefully into the space. She makes sure to bend down and allow the smudge to touch any shoes and other storage boxes on the floor of the closet, saying, "Clear the energy of all items in this closet from any negativity". Then she stands straight up once again and moves the Sage and Smudge along the line of clothing hanging there, repeating her affirmation.

She notices that several times during this process, the smoke seems to want to waft out into the room, or sink down towards the floor, instead of rising towards the ceiling inside the closet. At times like that she faces directly into the closet, and gently moves the wand from left to right, then stands still for a moment until the smoke rises straight up. This lets her know that any negativity or doubtful energy has been cleared from that particular garment. She notes the clothing near where the smoke had changed its pattern of movement, and thinks about situations where she might have encountered negativity while wearing it. Out loud, she says, "Let me benefit from the learnings of this situation. Clear and heal the energy surrounding this experience."

Finishing with the closet she continues to the third corner of the room, and once again facing towards the center of her bedroom, she holds out the wand and repeats her affirmation for the room. She now focuses her attention on the bed and the bed tables along this wall.

At the bed, she carefully pulls back the covers as if to make it ready for the night, and moves the wand over the place where she sleeps. She holds the ceramic bowl carefully under her glowing wand with her other hand, to make sure that no ash falls into the bedclothes. As she does this, moving around the bed and clearing the energy on all sides of it, she says, "Remove any negative energy from this place of rest. May I and any other sleeping in this place sleep well. May we know healing from any stress encountered during the day, and may we waken revitalized. May any dreams prove helpful and offer clarity. May we be filled with abundant energy, ready to welcome all benefit from our daily life."

Watching the smoke rise directly above the bed for a moment, she then turns carefully and continues her ritual. Now she clears the nightstand near where she sleeps - so no negative vibrations remain attached to anything standing on it or placed in its drawers. Since this is the piece of furniture in the room that is closest to her while she is sleeping, she pays extra attention to the movement of the aromatic smoke as she clears the energy of the space. Then she continues around the edges of the bed, and reaches the other nightstand, applying her attention to it as well before continuing to the fourth corner of the room. She stops there once again, facing out into the room and holding her wand pointed towards the center of the room. Once again she repeats her affirmation for the room.

Continuing her way she stops to clear the energy of the chair that is placed near the doorway to her bedroom, and observes that the smudge sinks into the space where she normally sits to dress or undress. She notices the continued downward movement of the smoke, and out loud she says "I ask that this chair may be cleared of any stressful energy that may have remained in my body after my day away from this place. Cleanse and clear any negative energy from this space". Satisfied that the smoke is once again rising into the air, she looks around.

Now, having completed her circle of the entire space, and having Saged, Smudged, and Cleared all of the furniture and things in the room, she moves towards the "center" of the bedroom and stands still for a moment, watching the smoke rise from her Sage Wand.

Holding the wand at the level of her heart, she breathes in the aromatic scent of the Sage - consciously - three times. Then with her mind on her purpose, she affirms once again: "May this room provide a safe place for me and for those I love. May comfort and ease abound in this space, and may we sleep here both soundly and well, and awaken with fresh enthusiasm to meet every new day. Bless this space with peace and bless me. May there be only harmony and comfort here."

Finally, looking around the room, she pronounces the room cleared and cleansed. She walks out the doorway to the ceramic pot with sand she had placed there before she started her Sage and Smudge ritual, and pushes the glowing end of the Sage Wand into the sand and waits until she sees no more smoke rising from it. She will carry the wand to the kitchen and dip it in some water to make sure that all of the embers are out.

This is her personal ceremony, her own Sage and Smudge Ritual for clearing her personal space. This is smudging.

One of the first and most important rooms to clear and heal as you start working with sacred smoke is the room where you sleep. Your psyche, your dreams and your connection to the spirit world rejuvenate you and strengthen your soul for its journey through life each day. So it is extremely necessary for you to be aware of the energy levels in your bedroom, to make sure that the energy in the room "feels" supportive to your life's purpose. Any time you feel even the slightest discomfort or uneasiness in your life in general, take a little time to assess the energy levels in your bedroom to make sure that nothing is amiss in that space.

If you share your sleeping space with a lover, a husband, your child or a pet, you need to be aware that less than pleasant happenings may have occurred in their lives during the time you were not with one another during the day. And as you sleep, any disturbing energies either you or your loved ones have encountered during the day are released into the space where you are sleeping and can

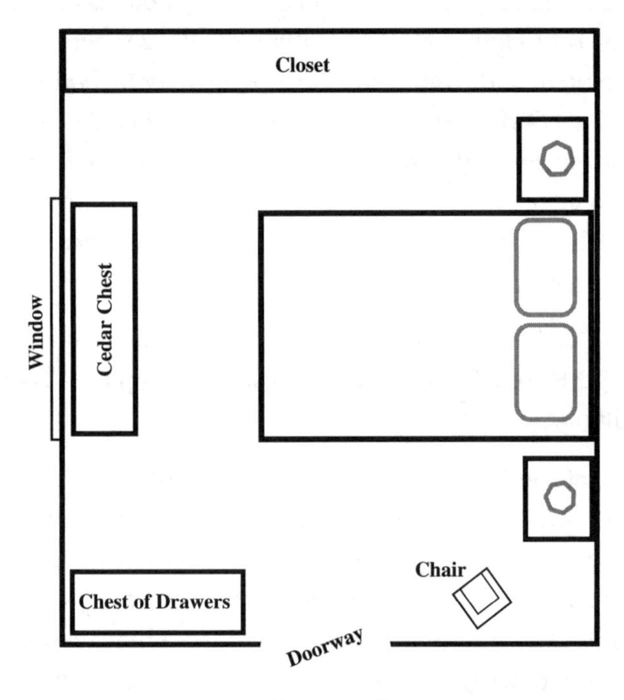

Diagram 1

become part of the "current" of influences that flow through the room while you are in the dream state.

It is very important to keep your bedroom free of any negative influences, so that you and whoever shares your space at night can awaken refreshed and ready to live your best lives each day! If you are going through a difficult time at work or in your relationships, you need to be especially aware that the energy of the stress and challenges you are facing when you are awake becomes even stronger when you sleep. So, especially during times of stress in your life, you will want to carry out a Cleansing and Clearing Ritual in your bedroom on a regular basis.

The example of a bedroom clearing that you find at the beginning of this chapter takes place in the bedroom shown in Diagram 1. You may want to read through this description of a Personal Sage and Smudge Bedroom Clearing ritual once again, referring to the diagram as you read it, so that you are quite familiar with the general process of carrying out a Personal Sage and Smudge Clearing. Then, when you are ready, you might want to get out your personal journal so you can make an outline of the steps you want to take to clear your own bedroom of any negative energy! You will find it helpful to refer to both Diagram 1 and Diagram 2 as you continue reading this chapter.

To Think About...

When you are planning to clear your bedroom of negative or stressful energy, think about whether your bedroom is attached to a bathroom, or to a walk-in closet. These are additional areas than can "collect" negativity, and you need to plan to spend a little time in each of them separately as you clear the space, almost as if they were "separate rooms".

Some people prefer to shower at night before bed. Many people take a shower in the morning - but they may crawl in bed at night without showering, knowing they will bathe the next morning. In some cases, when you share your bedroom with another, their bathing routines/customs and your own differ. It is, however, particularly advisable to shower at night if you are going through a lot of stress on a personal level, or spend your time in stressful environments during the day! If you and your partner have different bathing rituals, see below for Personal Clearing suggestions.

Showering removes the energy you may have "collected" during the previous hours. Any feelings and emotions you may have momentarily registered during the day, conversations, challenging (or pleasing) interactions with others, experiences and responses of every possible nature - all leave their "energetic imprint" on you. If these have been good experiences, then the problem is minimized. However, it is not always possible to know if, during the course of the day, you have encountered someone who is going through a difficult time in their own lives!

The clothing you wear also picks up the vibrations of the people you have spent time with and the places you have visited during the day. If you clothes hamper is located in the bedroom, the closet or a connecting walk-in closet or bathroom, it may be necessary to pay particular attention to that area of your sleeping environment.

Where do you keep your shoes? Usually people keep them in their closet in the bedroom, and most people do not thoroughly clean their shoes every day. Usually people simply take them off, and place them back in their place in the closet until the next time they want to wear that pair! If this is part of your routine as well, know that a great deal of the energy you consciously or unconsciously encounter in your world as you go about your daily life is brought into your personal space through your outer garments and your shoes. The energy these articles of clothing collect during the day while you wear them is transferred to and stored in your closet and can subsequently affect your quality of life.

Tips and Tools

Some people keep little sachets with bits of Sage, Cedar, Juniper, Rosemary, Thyme or Lavender in their closets and in the bottom of the clothes hamper to clear negative energy on a continual basis. This is a good idea, and you can place dried Lavender under your bed or in your pillowcase, or in the drawers where you keep your nightclothes, so the energy of the Lavender (which is renowned for restoring balance and creating a peaceful atmosphere) is around you as you sleep. (It might even be a good idea to have a little sachet of Lavender or one with Sage and Lavender with you when you travel or plan to sleep away from home at a hotel or in someone else's home as their guest - just to ensure that you are protected and sleep well when you are away from your home!)

If you know that you are going through a stressful period in your life, or if you know that your partner or someone who shares your bed is going through difficulties, it is a good idea to smudge your sleeping quarters often during such a time. Some people smudge briefly morning and evening and keep a shell and small containers or jars with loose White Sage and Lavender in the bedroom. They put a little of the White Sage and the Lavender in the shell and light their smudge, creating sacred smoke for a short time in the morning, and again in the evening before going to sleep. They say it calms their nerves and they sleep better!

Simple Bedroom Clearings

A brief Bedroom Clearing Ritual for creating a peaceful atmosphere, drawing in loving energy and helpful spirits requires that you either have a Sage and Lavender Wand, or loose Sage and Lavender and a container or vessel (in which to burn them) at your disposal. Plan to spend a few minutes performing a short ceremony before you go to bed.

If you use a wand, light it, and wait until the aromatic smoke is rising steadily. Stand comfortably in the "middle" of your bedroom with your feet slightly apart, and hold your wand in your left hand at the level of your heart. Spend a few moments facing each of the four walls in the room. Then stand still, allowing the smoke to move around the room as it will, saying your clearing and cleansing words for the room in general, and stating your affirmations for peace and protection in the space. You might want to move briefly to the closet and open it to allow some smoke to enter, or take a brief moment to walk into a walk-in closet or an attached bathroom. Allow the smoke rising from the wand to carry its message to all corners of your personal space.

Then douse the wand in water or put it - top down - into somc sand to extinguish the embers smoldering inside the wand. If you use water to put out the embers in your smudge wand, dip the wand into the water for a brief moment, then lift it out and place it on a plate to dry in a safe place in your bedroom until the next time you want to use it for a Sage and Smudge Bedroom Clearing. If you extinguish the burning embers in a container filled with sand, leave the wand top down in the container, and place it (the container with the wand in it) in a safe place in your bedroom before going to bed. (You want to make sure that the wand is "buried" at least halfway in the sand, so that any embers that may be burning in the wand cannot continue to do so after you have completed your Bedroom Clearing.)

If you use loose herbs for your Sage and Smudge Bedroom Clearing, you may want to keep some of the herbs you like to burn in your bedroom at all times. Then you can simply take some of them, place them in a heat-resistant container or vessel when you are ready to start. Use either a small charcoal brick, lighting it and adding the herbs, or light the herbs directly with a match. White Sage on its own, or crushed White Sage and Lavender are good choices for this type of clearing. Think about whether you want to hold the vessel as you carry out your clearing (it will become very hot if you use a charcoal brick to light the herbs), or if you want to place it on a piece of furniture in the bedroom. If you are not going to hold the vessel during your clearing, then set up your "Sacred Smoke place" in the room as described in Chapter 5.

If you are going to hold the vessel with the smoking Sage and Smudge herbs (see Chapter 5), follow the suggestions for carrying out a Sage and Smudge Bedroom Clearing in a similar manner as the one described above for the use of a wand. You may want to start your ritual using a feather or a fan to use to waft the smoke first up towards the ceiling, and then into the four corners of the bedroom. Then you can proceed around your space, using the feather to move the smudge in the direction of the furnishings, inside your closet and any connecting spaces.

You will definitely want to have a feather or a fan to use if you have placed your vessel with the smoking Sage and Smudge herbs on a piece of furniture in your bedroom, to make sure that the smoke is moved in all directions as you carry out the clearing.

Don't forget to fold back your bed linens, open any closet doors, and waft some smoke in that direction, or to move the smoke into an attached bathroom with quick movements of the feather or the wand. To conclude your ritual, stand still in the "middle" of your space, allowing the smoke to move around the room as it will, saying your clearing and cleansing words and affirmations for the room in general, specifically asking for peace and protection in the space.

Before you finish your smudge ritual, make sure that the smoke rises upwards on its own. If necessary, stand still, repeating the words you use for your ceremony until it does so. Then you will know that the space has been completely cleared of any negative energy. When you are finished with your Sage and Smudge Bedroom Clearing, allow the herbs to simply burn out on their own.

Personal Clearing

You may want to smudge yourself before going to bed as well. During your Sage and Smudge Bedroom Clearing, include a Personal Clearing for yourself. Breathe in the essence of the sacred smoke herbs, and focus on yourself and your body for a moment, then bend and allow the wand or the feather (or fan) to move the smoke down as far as possible, to your ankles and feet. Move the smoke from that position near the floor slowly up the length of your body to the top of your head. This helps to cleanse your aura of any disturbances you may have experienced that day.

Finish your Personal Clearing, holding the wand or the feather in front of you at the level of your heart, and watch the sacred smoke rising up. Repeat any affirmations you say for your own well-being and spiritual purpose. Breathe again deeply, and then complete the ritual. Now you can rest. Now you will sleep comfortably and your dreams will be undisturbed.

Complete Bedroom Clearing

Once a week, during especially stressful times, you will want to carry out a Complete Bedroom Clearing, similar to the one described in the opening paragraphs of this chapter. Start by taking out any laundry from your bedroom (or any attached closet or bathroom where it collects during the week). Change the sheets and clear the room of any mess that may have accumulated since the last time you did such a clearing. Vacuum, dust and prepare the bed as if you were going to sleep in it. (Pull back the covers so the sheets are open out to the room.) Open each drawer just a few inches, and open the closet doors, so your clothing and shoes are visible when you stand in the "center" of your room. If you have an attached bathroom or a walk-in closet, open these doors as well, so there is a flow of energy in the space.

Take a few moments to select the sacred smoke herbs you will use and gather your tools. Good selections of sacred smoke herbs for this type of ritual will include a White Sage Wand or Sage Stick, or a Sage and Lavender Wand or Stick, and possibly a vessel with a charcoal brick. You might want to burn some Mugwort or Rosemary in the vessel at the same time you walk around your space with the wand in your hand. The Mugwort or Rosemary are especially good for this kind of clearing, since they help stimulate dreams, drive away evil spirits and negativity, and protect boundaries.

Start your Complete Bedroom Clearing and Healing Sage and Smudge Ritual by lighting the charcoal brick in the vessel, and placing some crushed herbs on it. Let them start smoking, then go and stand at the entrance door to your bedroom. Observe the open drawers, the welcoming bed, the open closet and, if you have an attached bathroom, the entrance to the bathroom.

Holding the Sage and Smudge Wand in your left hand, light it and wait a few moments at the doorway to make sure that your smudge stick or wand will continue to smoke when you start moving around. Keep the lighter with you (a pocket is a good thing!) in case the smoke stops, and the wand needs to be lit once more. If your wand does stop smoking, stand in that place, re-light the wand and remain still for a few moments to observe if the smoke is rising up towards the ceiling before continuing your ritual or clearing.

In this Bedroom Clearing you will move counter-clockwise around the room, around the furniture in the room, making sure that you allow the smoke to be a signal to you when you need to focus a little more of your energy and concentration on a particular area. If the smoke is

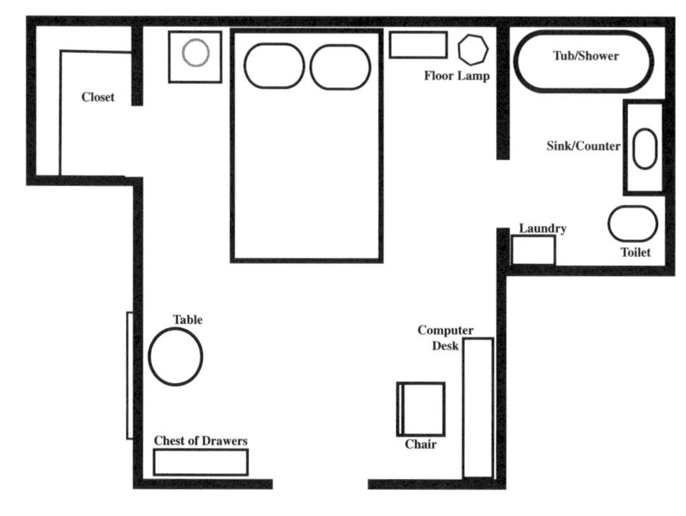

Diagram 2

very "thin", and little energy seems to come from your wand, apply the lighter again, until you see a thicker amount of smudge energy rising from the wand. Follow, as closely as you can, the ritual described at the beginning of the chapter.

If your bedroom is more like the one in Diagram 2, you will need to thoroughly smudge the walk-in closet and/or bathroom when you are clearing the wall with the door that leads into those areas from your main sleeping area. In this diagram, for example, after facing into the center of the bedroom from the third corner of the bedroom, you come to the bathroom door. At that point you would need to enter the bathroom to clear it before continuing with your Complete Bedroom Clearing along the third wall.

You would enter the bathroom; keep moving in a counter-clockwise fashion in this "new" space and begin to clear the area directly to the left inside the bathroom door. When you arrive at the tub/shower, focus on moving the wand over the area where you bathe. Be very clear about smudging away any negativity or other unwanted energy from your tub or shower area - remember that this is where the unwanted energy that has collected around you during the week has been washed from your physical body. You might want to say, "Clear and remove any negative energy from this space.", as you smudge this area.

Now continue along the next wall, clear the sink and counter area, the toilet and then clear any other storage areas in the bathroom. Before leaving the bathroom, stand in the center of it and say, "Cleanse and purify this space of all negative and stressful energy. Bless this space and all who spend time in it." Then continue out of the bathroom, and complete the Bedroom Clearing along the remaining third wall of the bedroom.

As you come to the bedroom door, stop at the door, then go to stand in the "center" of your bedroom to complete the clearing ritual. Repeat your affirmations for the room out loud three times. You might finish by saying, "I call blessings of love, joy, comfort and well-being into this space."

It is quite sufficient to spend 5-10 minutes on the

actual Sage and Smudge part of your "Whole Bedroom Clearing Ritual". When you have completed your clearing, put out the embers of your Sage and Smudge Wand in some water, then close the drawers, make up the bed, close the closet doors and the bathroom door and set the Wand to dry until the next time you use it. Know you will be ready for a good sleep tonight!

If the aromatic smoke is too intense in any area of your bedroom, you can open the window or a door to allow the smoke to escape into the air outside. If your clothing or towels retain too strong a scent from the Sage and Smudge after you have completed your clearing, you can hang them outside in the fresh air for 20-30 minutes and allow them to "air out" a little before placing them back in your closet.

One of the best things about this ritual is the sense of peace that accompanies the process - a peace that will continue to bless your personal space for quite some time. If you are not going through a particularly stressful time in your life, it is not necessary to do a Complete Bedroom Clearing as often. In that case, try doing one at the time of the New Moon each month to help you focus on bringing more love and happiness into your life.

Chapter 8

Clearing and Healing Your Home Environment

The Sage and Juniper Wand he has chosen for his process this evening is about 10 inches long, and just a bit over an inch thick. He has selected a powerful tool for the House Clearing Ritual he has been planning ever since he was lucky enough to buy the condominium from a friend who is moving out of state. The wand is tightly wrapped with the dark red and royal blue thread he chose to represent his focus this evening. He wants his condominium to serve both as a home for himself and his cats, and as a base for the web design business he has been building the past three years.

He thinks about the assortment of Sage and Smudge tools he is carrying with him this evening, and glances up at the night sky to observe that indeed, no Moon lights the heavens. He chose the New Moon for this House Clearing because his new home will serve as a "fresh start" following the completion of his divorce some months ago. He bends down and places a planter filled with sand just outside the threshold to the front door. Placing his briefcase filled with Sage and Smudge tools down as well, he checks his pocket for the green cigarette lighter he likes to use - yes, it's right there.

Sitting in his car before approaching the door of his new home, he has looked over the pages in his journal where he had written down his thoughts about the Sage and Smudge Ritual he is about to perform. He briefly reminds himself of the details of the floor plan of the home he is getting ready to clear. He bends down to open his briefcase and pulls out his Sage Wand and the key to his new home. Then standing upright once again facing the door, he uses his right hand to unlock the front door, his first time as the new owner of the space.

The heavy wooden door swings inwards. He extracts his key but leaves the door unlocked. Next he reaches for his lighter to light the Sage wand. He grasps the wand firmly in his left hand as he lights the end of his Sage wand, and waits until the flame burns some of the threads that bind the wand before returning the lighter to his pocket.

The flame flares brightly, lighting up the space around him. He waits for a few moments to see that the Sage leaves remain lit before blowing gently on the end of the wand to encourage the fire to start burning within the wand itself. Bending down to his opened briefcase once again, he pulls out a flat brown ceramic plate. It's the one he always uses to catch any ash or burning herbs that might fall from the wand as he moves around performing his Sage and Smudge rituals. Good. The flame has become a glow, and smoke is rising thickly from the wand and straight up into the night air.

He wonders briefly what his new neighbors might think if they were to look out their windows and catch a glimpse of him behaving "so strangely". Will they imagine someone is breaking into the house? Will they call the authorities?

Will they come and disturb his process? Shaking his head as if to toss out these extraneous thoughts, he then focuses his entire attention on the smoke from the wand as it "enters" his new home with the help of a slight gust of wind from behind him. He wants to be sure to see which direction the smudge chooses to go when it gets inside, so he will know which direction to follow as he performs the House Clearing.

Ah, the smoke is drifting slightly to the right - so his process will be to follow a counter-clockwise movement through his home as he clears and heals the energy and blesses his new dwelling. Holding the Sage wand in his left hand, he reaches into his new home, placing the brown ceramic plate on the floor of the entryway with his right hand. With the same hand he switches on the light inside the front door. He lifts his briefcase and places it inside the door, opens it again and pulls out his journal. He opens it to the right page so he can read his first words, his first affirmations for his new home.

Now finally, stepping over the threshold and into the entrance hallway of his new home, he speaks out loud, addressing the energy all around: "Clear and cleanse any negativity and all disruptive energy from this home. I call blessings of love, joy, comfort, prosperity and protection into this space. Thank you for welcoming me as your new owner. I will take care of this home and be responsible for all that it needs. In return I ask that I be safe and comfortable for as long as I live here, and that this home provide a place of benefit for me and all who come to share and contribute to my life at my invitation."

Satisfied that he has stated his intent to the Universe, he steps around his briefcase, enters the house fully. He closes the front door, leaving the planter filled with sand outside to use to put out the fire burning in his sacred smoke wand at the end of his House Clearing Ritual.

With his back now to the closed front door, he looks to his right and sees the first doorway leading into the Guest Bathroom. He knows that many people have visited and spent time with the former owner, and this is one place he knows will be filled with all kinds of energy these people may have left behind them in the condo. Standing in the hallway and facing into the bathroom, he switches on the light there, and steps into the room, saying, "Clear this space of any negative energy." Then he carefully moves the Sage and Juniper Wand over the countertop, the sink and around the toilet area.

He is careful to open the cupboard doors under the sink and move the smudging wand into that space. He turns to face each wall in this narrow room as he clears the energy of the room. Back at the door, facing out into the hallway, he moves his Sage wand around the doorframe and repeats his affirmation for the Guest Bathroom, then leaves the room.

The next door is to a small den he will use as his office. Facing into the room he imagines where he will place his computer station, his bookshelves and file cabinets. He watches the smudge rising in the room, and states his affirmation for the space: "Clear this space of any negative energy. I ask that this office provide a place of creativity and success for me, and that all work done in this room bring benefit to my life and the lives of the people who receive my services. May satisfaction and abundance be the reward for my work!" He moves along the first wall, observing that the smudge from his Sage and Juniper wand continues to rise straight up towards the ceiling of the room.

At the first corner of the room, he faces out into the center of the space and repeats his affirmation for the office, and similarly he repeats his affirmation from each corner of the room. Finally, before leaving the den/home office, he moves to the center of the room. Standing tall and holding his Sage wand out about a foot from his chest, he talks to the room briefly, describing his business, mentioning highlights of work he has done in the past, and plans he has for the future as he watches the smudge continue to rise towards the ceiling. At last, moving to stand at the doorway facing out into the rest of his home, he moves the wand around the edges of the doorframe as he says: "Clear this space of any negative energy. Bring abundance and satisfaction from all aspects of my work." Then he moves on to the Master Bedroom.

This is the room where he will spend a great deal of personal time, so he has decided on a special affirmation for the room: "Clear any negativity that may have formerly been accepted and allowed in this space. I call blessings of love, joy, comfort, personal benefit and protection into this room." Continuing into the room and moving along to his right, he almost immediately arrives at the door to the Master Bathroom - which must be cleared now before he can continue the ritual in the bedroom.

He enters the bathroom, and performs his Bathroom Clearing ritual there, careful to spend a little extra time clearing the space where the bathtub is, to the left of the doorway. He notices that his wand is not smudging well, and reaches into his pocket for the lighter, and spends a few moments re-igniting the wand before continuing with his Clearing of the space.

Finishing up in his bathroom he re-enters his bedroom area once again, and makes his way along to the wall with the wall closet. He slides open these closet doors and carefully smudges inside, from floor to top shelves, making sure that all old energy is removed from the space, and imagining where he will place his things in the closet when he unpacks them in his new home. He adds a prayer for protection, since he will store some of the things that are valuable to him in this closet: "Protect all of my property stored in this space from anyone with evil intent! I call the energy of safety and security into this space."

As he moves towards the place where the former owner had her bed, he notices that the smudge from his wand seems to dwindle, and the smoke sinks towards the floor. Stopping there, he blows gently on the wand to encourage the embers to glow, waiting until the smudge rising from the wand thickens. When it does, he walks around the outline where the bed has been, affirming out loud, "Cleanse and clear any negative energy from this space. Remove any negative energy from this place of rest. May I sleep well in this room. May I know healing from any stress that enters my life and may I be filled with abundant energy as I sleep. May I wake up refreshed to start each new day!" Watching to see that the smoke from his wand continues to rise up towards the ceiling, he realizes that the negative energy he encountered there has been lifted, and he can continue.

At the next corner of his bedroom he turns and faces into the center of this room and waits again until the smoke from the wand rises up towards the ceiling. Then he continues along the final wall of the Master Bedroom, slowly moving the wand up and down as before, stopping to observe the movement of the sacred smoke as he does so.

Finally he reaches the door between the Master Bedroom and the rest of the living space, but before leaving the room he walks to center of it. Standing tall, holding the wand at chest level about a foot out from his body, he takes a few moments to talk out loud to "energy" or "spirits" in the room, saying, "In this room I will keep all of my personal clothing, my bed and my dresser. My pets are welcome to sleep on my bed. I want to sleep well in the room, dream positive dreams, and wake each morning with lots of energy to live my best life."

Still holding the Sage Wand at chest level, and watching the smoke rise into the air above him, he repeats his Bedroom Blessing one more time: "Cleanse and clear any negative energy from this space. Remove any negative energy from this place of rest. Protect all of my property stored here from anyone with evil intent! I call the energy of safety and security into this space. May I sleep well in this room. May I know healing from any stress that enters my life and my I be filled with abundant energy as I sleep. May I wake up refreshed to start each new day!" He proceeds into the living room.

As he looks around the room, standing directly outside his bedroom door, he repeats the words he said as he entered his new home: "Cleanse and clear any negativity and all disruptive energy from this home. I call blessings of love, joy, comfort, prosperity and protection into this space. Thank you for welcoming me as your new owner. I will take care of this home and be responsible for all that it needs. In return

I ask that I be safe and comfortable for as long as I live here, and that this home provide a place of benefit for me and all who come to share my life at my invitation."

He can see from the marks in the carpet where furniture had stood previously and makes a mental note to clear those areas with the smudge rising thickly now from his Wand. And he pays attention to the opening at the other end of the room to his left, the opening that leads into the kitchen. He thinks about the floor plan he studied in preparation for this House Clearing ritual, and now he is ready to proceed.

Turning right, he stoops down slightly to bring the smudge as close as possible to the floor as he considers this area of his home. There is a large glass window and sliding door that opens to the patio along the far wall of his condominium in this room. In front of it, and along the wall between his living room and bedroom, is the area where he will set his entertainment unit. He observes the far right corner of the room noting where the cable that will connect his television with the world outside pierces the floor and the carpet.

He watches carefully how the smudge is moving, and as he approaches the far wall (the first "corner" of his living room) he says, "May the cable that connects my world and the outside world bring me the information and communications I need. May I benefit from all communications entering and leaving this house."

Now he approaches the full window and the sliding door, stands at the right side facing it, and moves the smoking Sage and Juniper Wand along the edges of the window. He pays special attention to the window ledge and to the glass sliding door because he knows this is where his cats will sit to observe the world outside of their home, and he knows that this entryway to his home is possibly less secure than the front door.

He says, "Protect and guard this window and door opening from any persons or outside forces that might bring negative energy into my space, or force an entry to my home. May my cats enjoy the view from this place, and may the garden and patio area be filled with beauty and life." At the far edge of the sliding door he says, "May no harm enter through this door from the outside world. May all who are in the space be protected, and may all my possessions remain safe inside these doors. I call a guardian spirit to watch and protect my patio and garden, and this entrance to my home!"

Then he moves to stand in the second corner of his living room, turns facing out into the middle of the room and, holding the wand out a little at chest level, affirms: "I call blessings of love, joy comfort, prosperity and protection into this space. Clear and heal any negativity that may have been permitted here. Heal the energy of my living room."

He walks along the next wall of the room - the one that separates his condominium from the one next door; he moves slowly, observing the sacred smoke rising from his wand. He stops to clear the energy of the room any time the smoke from the wand sinks down towards the floor, or moves out and away from the wall. Every few steps, he stoops slightly to bring the smudge as close to the carpet as he comfortably can, and reaches as high towards the ceiling as he can, moving the wand slowly up and down as he walks along the length of the entire wall.

He cannot complete the living room ritual at this time, because the kitchen leads off the main room, and must be cleared first. The two areas, living room and kitchen, are not separated by a door that can be closed between them. So he knows he will have to complete his ritual for the living room after he has completed the clearing of his kitchen.

Since there is no real "third corner" in the living room, as he comes to the counter dividing the living room from the kitchen, he turns and faces into the living room and says, "Clear any energy from this area that does not benefit me and those I love, and cleanse all negativity that may remain from the past. I call blessings of love, joy, comfort, prosperity and protection into this space. May all who come here at my invitation feel at ease, comfortable in my home." Then he turns his attention to the kitchen area, preparing to continue the counter-clockwise path of his Sage and Smudge House Clearing Ritual around the counter and into the kitchen.

At the end of the counter, at the opening to his kitchen, he now faces into the kitchen. He carefully smudges the countertop to his right, then stands tall, and says, "Clear and cleanse any negativity or unhealthy energy from this space. I call blessings of love, joy, comfort, good health and wellness to reside in this kitchen space. May all that is prepared in this kitchen be to my benefit and the benefit of those living with me, and increase our well-being."

He continues into the kitchen, carefully opening every cupboard door, every cabinet, the drawers, sinks, dishwasher, stove and refrigerator, saying a special blessing for each of these spaces. He moves the wand along each countertop and over the cook top of the stove, and briefly turns on the fan above his stove to pull some sacred smoke up into it as well. At the edge of his kitchen, where the hallway to his right leads to the living room in front of him and to the entrance hall, den, guest bathroom and outer door, he stops, turns and faces into the kitchen once again. Holding the Sage and Juniper Wand at the level of his heart, he repeats the prayer for his new kitchen.

Then he turns to face the living room, preparing to complete his ritual in that space. Facing towards the center of the living room area, he repeats his blessing for the room and for the house: "I call blessings of love, joy, comfort, prosperity and protection into this space. I ask that I be safe and comfortable for as long as I live here, and that this home provide a place of benefit for me and all who come to share my life at my invitation. Clear and heal any negativity that may have been permitted here. Heal and clear the energy of my living room."

He walks to the center of the room, and standing tall, holding his Sage and Juniper Wand in his right hand, a few inches out from his chest, he takes a deep breath, inhaling the scent of the sacred smoke rising from the Wand. He looks around at each of the areas in the room, to the place where his entertainment unit will stand, and where the other furniture and artwork will be hung or placed.

He talks to the "energy" and the "spirits" he has called into the room with his Clearing ritual about the activities he will do there, and the feelings he wants to experience. He talks about his home business and the future he hopes to build in his new home. He talks about his friends, people who will be welcome in the space, and his cats - naming them and thinking about how it will be for them to live here.

Finally, satisfied that he has expressed his hopes and his vision of the future, as well as his plans for the home, he inhales the essence of the herbs he is burning once again, repeats the House Clearing and Blessing affirmation one final time, and moves to the front door. There he carefully smudges round the entire doorframe on the inside, repeating his affirmation for the house and calling on protection, safety and security in the new home - for his pets, for his possessions and for himself. He turns to face into the condominium, extending his right hand with the Sage Wand out into the hallway and his entire home.

He stands very quietly, breathing in the aromatic scent of the smudge, watching the sacred smoke rise straight up as if to tell him that his process is a successful one, that his home is cleansed, cleared and healed of any old energy, and is ready to welcome him to his new life there. He says a final blessing, "May this house provide a safe haven for me. May comfort, ease, good health and abundance fill my life. Bless this home with peace and bless me, the owner of this space."

Then he opens his front door, steps out onto the step outside his doorway and looks at the ceramic pot with sand he had set outside of the door at the beginning of the Clearing Ritual. Carefully, he bends over and puts the glowing end of the Sage and Juniper wand straight down into the sand. He has completed his Personal Sage and Smudge House Clearing ceremony.

The most complicated and lengthy sacred smoke ritual most people will ever engage in is the "Complete Clearing and Healing" of their home environment. This type of Sage and Smudge ritual or ceremony is most often done around the time people move into a new home, to clear out any negative energy that may have been a part of the lives of the people who lived there previously.

However, there are other occasions when it is appropriate to perform a major purification, a Clearing and Healing Sage and Smudge ritual for the entire residence. This type of spiritual "housecleaning" ritual is performed to acknowledge that one cycle has ended and to "announce" a new beginning - a starting point in your energetic, vibrational and spiritual connection to your world. And since your home is the "center" of your personal world, it is appropriate to clear the entire space and make it ready for the next cycle.

Here are some examples of times when it is appropriate to clear and cleanse the energy of your entire home:

- When someone new moves into the home to live with current members of the household, bringing their possessions (possibly their children and/or their pets) into the space.
- Following the completion of a major home improvement project.
- Following a Feng Shui consultation, and after any changes suggested by the Feng Shui Practitioner have been made to the interior (or exterior) of the home - changes that are meant to shift/improve the energy-flow inside the home.
- Following a divorce or separation, where one party has moved all of their possessions out of the mutual home and into a new home of their own.
- At the time of a major "life-change" for anyone who lives in the home (such as the birth of a child, a major career change, children leaving home for college or to live on their own, retirement, diagnosis of a chronic illness, etc.)

- Following a serious illness or death of someone (or a cherished family pet) who has lived in the home.
- Following a natural disaster (like an earthquake, fire or flood).

Whether you are buying a home, renting a home or moving into a "new" apartment or condominium, you will want to perform a Sage and Smudge Home Clearing ritual some time during the first month you are living in the new space - preferably around the time of the New Moon. If there is time between when you take possession of your new home, and the time your furniture and belongings are moved into the new home, you may want to do an initial Sage and Smudge ritual like the one described at the beginning of this chapter before your furniture and possessions arrive and you start unpacking.

If you are unable to carry out a "Complete House Clearing" before your furniture and possessions arrive at the new dwelling, or if you don't unpack everything the first month you are in your new home, you may want to perform an initial Home Clearing ritual like the one described above during the first month, and another after everything is unpacked and moved into its new space!

The full description of how to clear and heal your personal home environment at the beginning of this chapter takes place in the home shown in Diagram 3. You may want to read through this description of a Complete House Clearing and Healing Ritual once again, referring to the diagram as you read it, so that you are quite familiar with the general process of carrying out this type of Sage and Smudge ritual. Then, when you are ready, you might want to get out your personal journal and make an outline of the steps you would take to clear your own home of any negative energy! You will probably find it helpful to refer to both Diagram 3 and Diagram 4 as you continue reading this chapter.

To Think About...

When you consider buying or renting a house, an apartment or condo it is a good idea to learn what you can about the people who lived there previously. Ask the Real Estate Agent, Rental Agent or Landlord why the house or apartment is on the market. However, they do not always understand the reason for such a question, and may or may not give you the information you need. If it is possible to find out, it is always a good idea to know what kinds of things have happened in the space before you move into it - to help you know what kind of ritual to carry out to ensure that you derive the greatest benefit possible from your new living circumstances.

In general, it is nice to buy or rent a home where the previous owners have experienced success or advances in fortune. For instance: They have been so successful that they are moving because they can afford a new, larger home for themselves and their family. Or, they have been offered an excellent job opportunity in another city or state, and are moving to pursue increasing success in their lives. Or, the previous resident has met someone special, and is moving to be married and start sharing life with their partner in a new living space.

It is also common now for people to move out of their larger homes as their children launch their own lives in

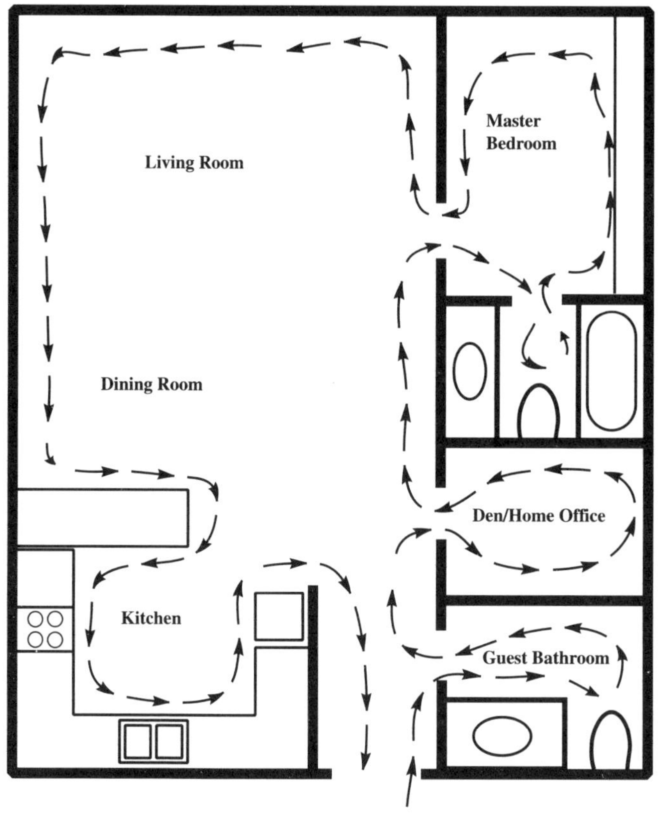

Diagram 3

other places. Perhaps the previous homeowners plan to move somewhere more suited for adult living or retirement. This lets you know that the house you may be thinking of buying or renting has provided a good and prosperous environment for a growing family in the past.

Even when you have been able to learn something positive about the previous residents, you will benefit from carrying out a Sage and Smudge ritual before you move into the home, to create your own energy field in the new dwelling. In some instances it is absolutely necessary to thoroughly smudge the home. The former owners may be moving due to a divorce, death, illness, loss of work opportunity and financial status, or some other sad occurrence in their lives. You don't want to move into the home without both removing the negative energy that has accumulated under that roof, and inviting in fresh and supportive energy for yourself and any others who will share the space with you!

Here is an example of a situation where a "Complete House Clearing and Healing" ritual was very necessary. Bob and his wife Cheryl found the perfect townhouse in a suburb of Los Angeles. They were very excited - it was the first home they had ever considered buying in their 10-year marriage. Both were doing well in their careers and felt ready to invest in their future home.

The residence they found sounded just perfect for their needs! It had a lovely living room with access to a spacious patio and a well-maintained small garden, a big kitchen opening into the dining area and to the patio, spacious Master Bedroom with a walk-in closet and private bathroom, and two smaller bedrooms (with a second bathroom in between) they would use for their home office and a guest bedroom. The size was just what they had been looking for, and the price was right. However, they learned that the previous owner had suffered a long illness and died of its complications.

Now obviously this townhouse had "enjoyed" the energy of the previous owner for many years. She had been the original owner, and lived in it with her husband for more than 20 years before he passed away and she succumbed to her illness. Asking a neighborhood resident about the house and the previous owners, Bob and Cheryl learned that they had been a very happy and popular couple in the community. Neither of the previous owners had passed away in the house; both had died in the hospital a few days after being taken there by ambulance.

When the Bob and Cheryl first saw the inside of the house they were going to buy, their initial impression was that it was "dark", it needed new paint and carpet, and some repair work. They thought that when these improvements were completed, it would be the perfect home for them.

There is often a "dark" feeling associated with houses where someone has been ill for a time. It is almost as if the home picks up the vibration of the people living in it, and when the people are not well or when they are unhappy the home has a "heavy" or "dark" feeling about it. Most people, when remarking on the impression they have about a home where some negative energy is present will say that "something doesn't feel quite right". They often imagine that paint, carpet, new lamps or some other repair project will improve the ambiance of the home. Home improvement projects, however, cannot disperse a "dark" or "negative" feeling.

In fact, the "feeling" in the house can best be improved by doing a thorough energy clearing; a Sage and Smudge ritual is ideal for this purpose! It is a good idea to carry out this kind of ritual before you make a decision about what kind of repairs or upgrades are needed. (It is possible you can save yourself considerable expense, as you might not need to do as many repairs or improvements as you think!)

While Bob and Cheryl were involved in the Escrow process of purchasing the home of their dreams, they began to put together a Sage and Smudge ritual to clear and heal the house of the current energy. They planned to draw beneficial support from the Universe for themselves and their home in the future.

Tips and Tools

It is always a good idea for two or more people (preferably people who are going to live together in the residence) to carry out a House Cleansing or Clearing and Healing Sage and Smudge ritual together. It can be difficult for one individual to manage all of the parts of the ritual on their own. However, if you are single and moving into a new apartment or house, you can invite a friend, family member or another person who is familiar with Sage and Smudge Clearing rituals to help you with your House Clearing. It is possible to perform the ritual on your own, but much more convenient if you have help!

Most people tell me that it feels like they receive "help" from the spirit world when they approach this type of ritual. It is important to remember that you are interacting with the energy of the Universe when you begin any ritual process, any ritual "work"! You will be "directed" and "shown" areas that require your particular attention.

If you are doing a House Clearing and Healing ritual on your own, it might be a good idea to set up a voice-activated tape recorder, and speak aloud when you notice certain phenomena. When you record your thoughts in this way you can rewind the tape later and listen to your own comments from the clearing ritual. Make notes in your journal of any thoughts that occurred to you while you were carrying out the initial Clearing. Then it will be easy for you to go back and do some more clearing work in areas that need special attention on future occasions.

If tape recording yourself seems difficult, you may want to bring a journal or pad of paper with you to use to take notes of the things you notice as you clear your personal space during a House Clearing ritual. If you are going to write down notes, you want to be able to pause in the process of your Clearing ritual. You will need a large fire-resistant plate on which you can temporarily put down your Sage and Smudge Wand when you need to stop for a moment and make some notes.

Jot down your impressions and thoughts as they occur to you during the House Clearing ritual. Take the plate and your journal with you as you carry out various aspects of the clearing. All in all, it is easier to do a Complete House Clearing when someone else is there to take notes, and draw your attention to things going on, to remind you if you miss something in the space - or forget some aspect of the ritual itself.

Sometimes, in circumstances like the one Bob and Cheryl encountered, where illness and death have been part of the energy of the house for several years prior to your moving in, it may be necessary to carry out the House Clearing Ritual more than once. They originally performed the Sage and Smudge House Clearing in the empty home before moving into it. For this first ceremony they chose a wand of White Sage and Cedar. These herbs are often combined in a smudge wand that will be used to purify people, places and things, to drive out negativity and negative emotions.

Bob and Cheryl then carried out a second Complete Sage and Smudge House Clearing after their things had been moved into the house. Using the notes they had taken during the first Clearing, they decided to carry a White Sage wand to smudge with throughout the whole House Clearing. And they chose to burn loose Rosemary and Thyme in two separate vessels, one placed in the center of the living room and the other in the kitchen where they had experienced a great deal of negative energy during the initial House Clearing ritual. (Rosemary and Thyme are often selected when people feel the need to protect themselves and their personal space.)

For this second aromatic smoke Clearing Ritual they also placed small wands made of Sage and Lavender in the bedrooms, and lit them when they entered these rooms in the process of their Complete House Clearing. They wanted to add a "cozy and relaxed" feeling to those areas, and to invite love and peaceful energy into these rooms. (Each Sage and Lavender wand was extinguished as they left the respective bedrooms, and kept for future use.)

Following the second House Clearing, the smoke from the Sage Wand they carried throughout the house during the ritual rose directly towards the ceiling in every area of the home. This indicates that all negative energy or spirits attached to the former residents had ultimately been cleared, healed, and released. The house was welcoming them and their energy to live there from that time on.

After clearing the whole home environment in this way, Bob and Cheryl were able to do "follow-up" rituals, calling in specific energy to various areas of the house as their belongings were unpacked and arranged. When everything was unpacked, they performed a third Sage and Smudge House Clearing using a Sweet Grass wand (or "braid") as they walked through the house. They also burned Rosemary in a half shell that was moved from room to room, placed in a central spot in each room as they walked around the edges of the rooms carrying the Sweet Grass. Both of these herbs created sacred smoke to bring positive energy into the environment.

Their third ritual took only 15 minutes, and the smoke rose readily straight up in each area of the whole townhouse. Bob reports that their life is prosperous and happy. They very much enjoy their new home and are glad they took the time to carry out these various rituals. Bob also reports that he has begun a habit of performing Sage and Smudge rituals on a regular basis at the time of the New and Full Moons as a compliment to other spiritual activities, and that he feels the energy flowing in his life is very positive.

Below is an outline you can use to plan Sage and Smudge Clearing and Healing Rituals for your home. You may want to carry out similar rituals to the ones described above if you are planning to move into a house or apartment. You may also want to carry out a House Clearing ritual if you are going through any of the other types of experiences listed earlier in this chapter. And it is a very good idea to plan a House Clearing and Healing Ritual if you have not performed one previously in your home, or you have been unable to obtain information about the previous owners or residents who lived in the space before you moved into it!

Take time to study a floor plan of your home, to outline your Sage and Smudge House Clearing in detail. First smudge the home with a Sage Wand (preferably one made with Desert Sage or White Sage leaves) in order to drive out negative energy, spirits or influences, and to invite in the energy and support you want for your life (and the lives of others who share your space). This is always a most important first step in clearing and healing a home environment!

Be prepared to carry out a "follow-up" Sage and Smudge ritual with a second smudging using the White Sage or White Sage and Juniper wand once again. Or smudge choosing a combination of sacred smoke herbs in different areas of the home.

Sweet Grass is one sacred smoke herb you may want to consider for smudging in the common areas of your home, especially the kitchen, dining room, living room and guest bathroom(s). Sweet Grass is used to affirm the presence of positive energy in the house after the negative ones have been banished following your initial Sage and Smudge House Clearing.

Use a combination of Sage and Lavender in the bedrooms, taking special care with the Master Bedroom. sacred smoke from Sage and Lavender helps to restore and maintain balance and create a peaceful atmosphere. These herbs draw loving energy to the room where you will spend a great deal of personal time (or intimate time with your partner). It is always important to safeguard the space in a house where you spend time in the sleep state, a state where you are most open and vulnerable to the energies around you!

Use a combination of Sage and Rosemary, Sage and Thyme or Sage and Mugwort to smudge the area that is going to serve as a home office, or one where you will handle the financial responsibilities (pay the bills, keep track of your finances and plan for investments or future expenditures). If you like, you can smudge with Frankincense as well, or Copal. These two have historically been burned to increase wealth and attract financial benefit. (Copal or Frankincense also support all kinds of creative work, so it can be a good idea to burn one or the other in rooms where you focus on the creative process, family activities, hobbies and home businesses.)

General Outline for a House Clearing and Healing Ritual

At the pre-determined time, open the front door of the house. If you can, stand outside and light your Sage Wand. If you cannot, step over the threshold and light your wand just inside the entrance area to the home.

When you see steady smoke rising from your wand, look to see if the smoke drifts to the right or to the left as it enters the dwelling, if it is drifting straight out into the entrance of the home in front of you or if it moves into the open air behind you, away from the residence.

If the smoke is drifting to the left, then start your House Clearing ritual in that direction, holding your smoking Sage wand in your left hand. The energy of the Sage and Smudge is indicating that it wants you to move in a clockwise direction.

If the smoke drifts to the right, you are being invited to move in a counter-clockwise manner throughout the home as you perform the ritual, and to hold the Sage Wand in your right hand as you carry out your ritual.

If the smoke is drifting out ahead of you and into the entranceway, or straight up and above you, or over and behind you (as if it is attempting to escape the home) know that you will have to move through the house first in a counter-clockwise (right) direction, then in a clockwise (left) manner, because much energy will be needed to clear and heal the space!

> ***Note: While you can close the front door, do not lock it or Sage and Smudge the entrance door or entrance area at this time. Move into the home to commence your ritual. You need to allow the "entry-way" to your home to be "unblocked" so the energies you are clearing from the home can find their way out!***

As you start out in the first space or the first room, state your purpose for the House Clearing in general and then say a little prayer for that space. Clear any negative energy (or spirits) by asking them to leave the space. If you do this "out loud", it makes more of a statement to the Universe!

Now move slowly towards the first door or entrance-way leading into the rooms of the house. Walk with measured steps in the direction you will follow throughout the ritual. Your "path" is to walk around the rooms, following the edge of the floor throughout the entire residence. Hold your Sage Wand first down as low as you comfortably can towards the floor, and then lift it as high towards the ceiling as you comfortably can as you walk around the inner parameter of your home.

Keep an observant eye on the movement of the smoke. It is best if the smoke rises straight up, following the line of the wall towards the ceiling. If it is not doing so in some area, take a step or two back into the room. Stand still and face the wall, move the wand from left to right a couple of times, saying: "Clear any negative energy from this space. Bring blessings and peace to this room." then stand still again watching the direction of the smoke.

Repeat this exercise until the sacred smoke rises straight up towards the ceiling. (Keep windows closed, heater or air conditioning and all fans off while you are carrying out your Sage and Smudge rituals. This makes it easier to observe the natural movement of the smudge from the wand.)

If the wand should go out at any time as you are walking around the room or the smoke become very "thin", stop where you are, and ask whatever energy (or spirit) is there now to LEAVE: "Clear any negative energy from this space. Bring blessings and peace into this room." Re-light your Sage Wand, observe the direction of the smudge, and when it rises, continue.

If the room that you are clearing has a door that can be shut (closing off the room from the rest of your home), you can complete the Clearing Ritual in the room before you continue on to clear the rest of the home.

This is how to proceed:

As you go around the four walls of the room, clear each corner, clear around the windows, inside of closets, cupboards or built-ins. As you come back around to the doorway, stop for a moment, turn and face into the room, and then go and stand in the center of the room.

Hold your Sage Wand out a little from your body at the level of your heart. Standing in the center of the room, watch to see if the smoke from your Sage and Smudge wand rises towards the ceiling. If it does not, say "Clear and remove any negative energy from this room. I call blessings of love, joy, comfort and well-being into this space and ask for protection from any harm." Breathe in the scent of the sacred smoke and wait to see if the smoke now rises up. (Repeat the affirmation if necessary, until the smudge rises above you.)

Next, still holding your Sage Wand out from your chest at the level of your heart, turn and look at each area of the room. It is time to think about what you will be doing in the room, how you want to feel when you are in the room, or what you hope to bring into your life (or the life of a loved one) as a result of spending time in this room.

If you are carrying out the Clearing Ritual with a partner, it is time for them to join you and stand with you at the center of the room and recite the Clearing and Blessing you have formulated for this room, to talk about what you both want to experience in the space. This allows "Spirit" to bring in the energy you wish to experience. Now is the time to say the prayer you have prepared for this room to invite the beneficial energy and spirits you are calling into your new home, and into this room in particular.

So, for instance, if you are in the kitchen - before going into the dining room - stop for a few moments and talk about what you are planning to do in your kitchen. Maybe you need to talk about diet and what kinds of activities will happen there. What meals will you prepare in the kitchen? Who will eat them? Perhaps you will only have breakfast at home. Or maybe you are planning to entertain a lot in your new home, and the kitchen will be used to prepare fun feasts! Perhaps you want to learn more about food and nutrition, and you will spend time at a table in the kitchen studying. Or maybe are planning a new diet and exercise regime. This is the time to talk about all of these things so the “kitchen gods” know what to expect and prepare for while you live in the home!

Then, when you have completed your work in the room to your satisfaction, and you see the sacred smoke rising into the air straight above you, it is time to move into the next room or space. At the entrance to each room step into the room facing the direction you have determined to follow throughout the house. (If you start by moving to the right, move right in each room).

As you do the clearing work in each room, walk along the walls, holding the Sage Wand down as low as you comfortably can, then lifting it up as high as you comfortably can, keeping an observant eye on the movement of the sacred smoke.

It is best if the smoke rises straight up and follows the line of the wall towards the ceiling. If you find yourself in the kitchen, a bathroom or other room with built-in fixtures, be sure to move the wand inside all of the drawers, cupboards, shelves or openings and ledges to clear any energy that may be trapped in them, and cleanse them for your purposes.

Continue in this manner throughout the rooms of the house. Make sure to clear each space of any negative energy, to repeat the blessing you have prepared for the house as a whole, and address a prayer asking for specific benefit in each room.

Remember to "clear, cleanse and ask for protection or positive support" at each window, in each closet, bathroom, cupboard or built-in. As you clear these spaces in each room, be sure to think about which of your possessions will be placed in them, how you will utilize the space.

Even if you are performing a Clearing and Blessing Ritual on your own, have a little "conversation" or state your expectations about the future. Do this part of the ritual as you stand in the center of each room/area before leaving the room to clear the next area of your home.

Sometimes the area/space/room you are clearing does not have a door you can close to separate the room from the rest of the residence. Then you will need to carry out the final "clearing and conversation work" in the middle of these spaces as you come back around the parameter of your home on your way to the front door once again. (You can see an example of this type of open floor plan in the entry-way, kitchen, dining and living room areas of Diagram 4.)

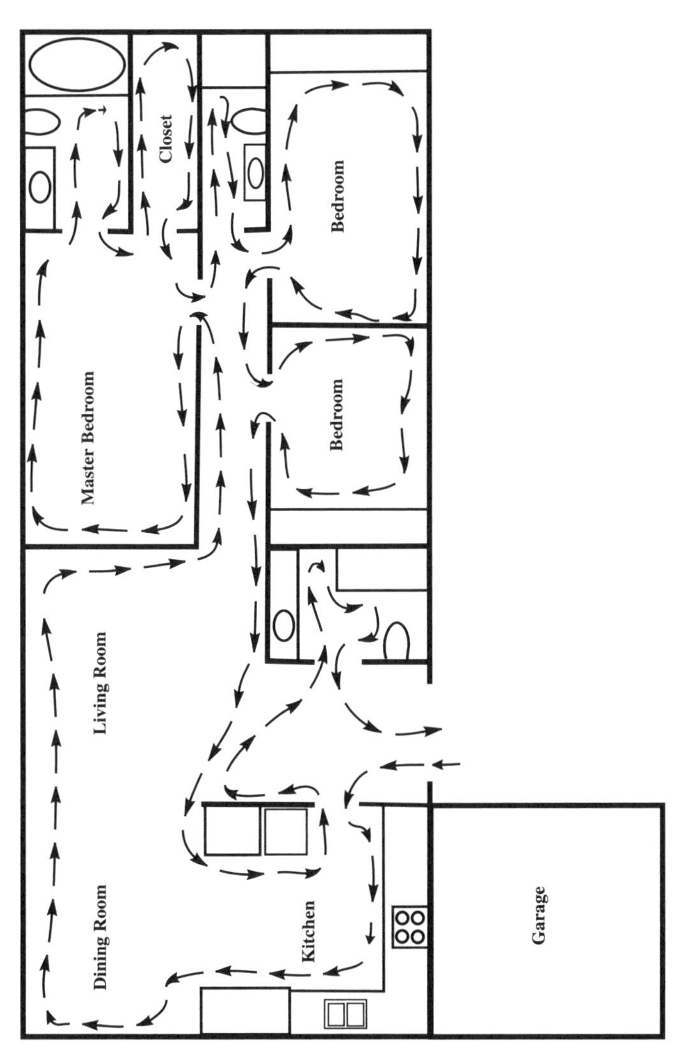
Closet
Bedroom
Master Bedroom
Bedroom
Living Room
Dining Room
Kitchen
Garage

Diagram 4

And sometimes the only way to get to a particular room or area of your home is to go through another room that is connected to it. For instance, in Diagram 3, it is not possible to enter the Master Bathroom without going through the Master Bedroom.

If you have connecting "rooms" like this in your home, you need to clear all attached rooms before you can complete the clearing of the main room. Always carry out your clearing ritual of the connected room(s) in the direction that will allow you to continue moving left or right, clockwise or counter-clockwise throughout the entire home. (For example, study the arrows on Diagram 3 indicating the direction that should be followed while clearing the Master Bathroom and re-entering the Master Bedroom to complete the clearing of the entire space.)

If you have only been able to clear "half" or part of a space in your home before proceeding on to the next connected room, you will clear the other "half" as you complete the House Clearing Ritual on your way back through the home. Only as you are clearing this "return half" is it appropriate to complete the Sage and Smudge ritual for each "room" by "standing in the middle" of them before proceeding on to the next "room" or living area.

If several living areas of your home are part of an open floor plan, you may choose to stand in the center of a multiple-use area to complete this part of the clearing. For example, the kitchen/dining/and living room areas are interconnected in Diagram 3. In the introduction to this chapter the owner of the condominium performed the "claiming, blessing and conversation" part of the ritual for the Dining and Living Room areas simultaneously. You can do likewise when you have an open floor plan as part of your living space.

In instances where there are no doors to close between living spaces, as you approach the first "passage-way" or "entrance" into the connected space in the house, move your Sage Wand from the floor, along the frame, wall or arch and clear your passage into the next room as you move into it. Then as you enter each "room" or "living area" in this manner, say a little prayer, asking that any negative energy (or spirits) in the space leave - in the manner described above (and in the opening paragraphs of this chapter).

As you come to each window, face the window, and move the Sage Wand around all of the sides, top and bottom of the window. Ask that no danger be allowed to enter the home through this window, and ask that the spirit world place a guardian by the window to protect you and your loved ones from harm. Ask that only positive energy enter the room from the world outside through the window. ("Bright light" and "clarity" are examples of good things to invite into your space through the windows of your home.)

Finally, as you come back to the front entrance to your home, stand for a moment facing into the home you have now completely cleared, cleansed and healed. Hold the Sage Wand at the level of your heart, breathe in the aroma of the sacred smoke, and ask if there is anything you need to know before you leave. Be still for a moment to see if any thoughts form in your mind, or any ideas occur to you.

Then affirm to the Universe that all former and non-beneficial energies, vibrations or spirits have now left the house, and that only beneficial and supportive spirits and energy are allowed to enter your home in the future.

Turn and face your front door. Move your Sage Wand around the doorframe, and stand for a moment in front of it, thinking about the feelings you want to have as you enter your home in the future. Think about the kinds of people who are welcome there, the kinds of activities you look forward to enjoying in your home.

Some people like to invite a "guardian" (or a Guardian Angel) to watch over the front of their home, as well as ones for each window and door or entrance-way into their home. This "guardian" energy or spirit will be responsible for protecting your home, all of the possessions and the people who live in it from any negativity. If you would like to do that, take a moment to do so before completing the Sage and Smudge House Clearing ritual.

At this point of the Clearing, look one last time to see the smoke rising directly above you, then open the front door, step outside, and extinguish your Sage and Smudge wand in either the water or sand you placed there for that specific purpose.

If it has been a very difficult House Clearing, one that has taken a lot of time and energy, you may wish to bury the remaining part of the wand in the earth. If your Clearing has taken a long time and your wand has burned down to within a couple of inches of the base, you may want to allow the wand to burn until it is completely consumed.

If at least half of your wand remains when you have completed your Clearing and Healing ritual, you can extinguish it in either the water or sand you placed outside your threshold for that specific purpose. Wait a few moments, then check to see that the embers in the wand are completely out. Dry out the wand (or tap out the sand it may have collected if you put out the fire in a container with sand) and keep it to use when you do other clearings in your home in the future.

After using Sage and smudging your entire home, you may notice that the more enclosed spaces of your home retain the scent of the Sage and Smudge for quite some time. If the scent of the herbs bothers you (or other members of the household), open the doors or windows for 15-20 minutes after smudging, to allow the smoke to air out. It may be necessary to "air out" your home several times, before the aromatic scent of the sacred smoke has entirely dissipated.

After such a complicated and time-consuming clearing, it is always a good idea to spend a little time writing down your thoughts, realizations and any observations in your journal. Keeping track of your clearings in a journal is helpful, because you can refer back to your notes at some point in the future. These notes can also be very helpful as you plan future clearing and healing rituals in your home to help maintain peace and harmony in your personal environment.

Chapter 9

Clearing and Healing Common Areas in Your Home

The White Sage Wand she holds in her left hand is about four inches long, and not quite an inch around at its thickest point. It is tightly wrapped at the base with a bright blue thread that continues to wind around the wand in the "diamond' pattern she so likes. In her right hand is the bright red lighter she prefers; it is set to light an inch of flame to hold to her Wand when she is ready to start her clearing in the dining room.

Every month for the past couple of years she and her friends have gotten together on the third Thursday evening of the month to enjoy dinner together, and then to discuss their creative writing projects. They listen to each other and offer suggestions or encouragement. This evening, however, she noticed that a couple of her friends were distracted and on edge. During dinner there had been a couple of "heated debates", and the energy in the room felt "strained" as they began their after-dinner exchanges.

As the meeting was drawing to a close she decided to Sage and Smudge the space after everyone had gone, to remove any negativity that might remain. She will use a particular type of wand she likes for a Clearing in her common areas, because it is bound with blue, a color that symbolizes "calm, cool reflection". Also, blue is her favorite color!

She looks around the dining room, and thinks about the places that she especially wants to clear, making a general outline in her mind of the clearing she is about to carry out. Then, holding the base of her wand firmly and lighting top with the flame from the lighter, she stands in the entrance-way to the room from the kitchen, and watches the smoke rise from the wand, diffusing in the air of the dining room she is about to clear.

Since the smoke doesn't indicate which direction to start (it is moving first to the right and then to the left), she decides to move around the room in a clockwise manner. So, turning to her left, she starts her clearing at the countertop that divides her kitchen and this space.

Stating her intention clearly, "Clear and remove any negative energy from this space!", she watches the smoke rising now towards the ceiling, and walks fairly quickly to the first "corner" of her dining area. Holding the wand at the level of her heart, just a few inches out from her chest, she faces towards the dining room table, and repeats her affirmation. Then she moves along the next wall, clearing the pictures hanging there, and the antique clock she found herself looking at several times during the meeting. The smoke rises and touches the face of the clock and wafts upward. Good. She moves towards the second corner of her dining room, faces out into the room once again and repeats her clearing words: "Clear and remove any negative energy from this space!".

Now she moves towards the table, and as she approaches it she observes that the smudge slows its movement, rising thinly from the wand, moving out from her body instead of towards the ceiling as it has up to this point. She re-lights the dried Sage leaves with the red lighter once more and waits until a flame burns brightly. She blows gently on the flaming end of her wand to encourage the fire to burn the herbs within the wand.

Then, as the thick sacred smoke rises once again from her wand, she approaches the first chair on that side of the table, turning it out from the table. Bending down, she moves the Sage Wand from side to side up along the back of the chair, under the chair and over the seat saying: "Cleanse and clear any negative energy from this chair and from this place at the table." She reaches the wand under the table as well to clear any negative energy that may have been "trapped" under it. Then she moves her Sage Wand over the area of the table that had been occupied by one of the members of the group during the meeting. She waits until the smoke rises towards the ceiling to indicate that any negative energy has now been cleared from the space. Moving around the table, she repeats her clearing process at each chair.

Only once more does she notice that the smoke from her Sage wand "sinks" towards the seat of the chair as she stands by it to clear the space. She concentrates on what she remembers about the person who sat there, and the conversation that took place during the meeting. Then, facing the chair she says, "Clear all negative energy from this chair. Help and heal my friend's spirit. May she find strength to manage the stress she encounters each day. The energy in this chair does not belong in my space. Clear all negative energy from this chair and from the room."

Then, waiting until the smoke from her Sage Wand once again rises towards the ceiling, she continues around the table clearing the remaining chairs. Finally, when she has made her way around the table, she reaches out her wand and holds it over the middle of the table, watching the smoke rise towards the lamp above the table. She stands still for a moment, breathing deeply three times and repeating her affirmation for the room, "Cleanse and clear any negative energy from this space."

She turns around and moves towards the wall behind her, then along this wall, clearing this part of the room as she continues to the third corner of the room. Standing there for a moment, holding the smudging Sage wand in front of her, she looks around the room to see if she has missed anything, and prepares to follow the fourth wall towards the entrance-way to the kitchen.

Before she starts her clearing of this part of the room, she bends down slightly, reaching her Sage Wand down towards the floor. Holding it a few inches from the wall, she watches the smudge rise steadily from the wand towards the ceiling. Then she moves on to clear the dining room window, careful not to touch the bright embers of her wand to the drapes or the shades she has drawn.

She observes that the smoke seems to waft out from the window and into the room. She opens the drapes and raises the shades and stands still for a moment, facing out into the night sky outside her dining room window. Then she sends a little prayer to her guardian angel: "Protect and guard this room. Clear and heal this environment from any outside energy that may have affected this space." She stands still for several moments repeating her prayer, and finally the sacred smoke rises towards the ceiling indicating that this area is now cleared of any negative energy.

She continues along the wall to the entrance-way to the kitchen where she turns and once again faces into her dining room while observing the smoke rising steadily from her wand. Now holding her wand at the level of her heart and out about a foot from her body, she once again thinks about the evening, the conversation, and her friends.

Out loud, she says, "Let me benefit from the learnings that have been shared this evening. Clear and heal the hearts of all who came together this evening around this table and in this room. Clear and heal the energy surrounding this experience. May this space provide a comfortable place for me and those who share it with me. Bless this space with peace and bless me. May there be only harmony and good friendship here."

She stands quite still, watching the sacred smoke rise towards the ceiling, concentrates on breathing in the aromatic scent - three times. Now the energy in the room "feels right" again, so she pronounces the room cleared, the space healed. She has completed her personal clearing ritual.

She turns around and walks to the kitchen sink, where she runs a little water over the tip of the wand for a few seconds to put out the burning embers within the wand. She places her dampened Sage and Smudge wand in a ceramic mug she uses for that purpose, and returns the lighter to the drawer where she keeps her Sage and Smudge tools.

She notices the little jar with ground sage in the drawer, and picks it up. She decides she will sprinkle a little of it on her "Welcome mat" outside the front door - just to affirm that her home is once again filled with peace, filled with the positive energy she loves to feel there. Ten minutes in all! Now she will enjoy the rest of her evening.

Some of the most common questions I hear from people who want to do their own Sage and Smudge rituals are about when it might be appropriate to carry out a Clearing or Clearing and Healing ritual for their homes. When I ask what has brought the question to mind, I am told that something doesn't "feel right" in some area of their house.

I remember a conversation I had with a friend on this very subject. Gail was feeling very uncomfortable in her living room. She often spent time in that room watching television and working on her hobby - crocheting afghans for her friends and family as Christmas presents, and to use as decorative swaths of color to place on her own furniture.

"Lately I have not wanted to take out my yarn and work on a project that previously was really exciting - a blanket for the baby my co-worker will have in October.", she told me. "I haven't even wanted to clean the bookshelves in the room, and I no longer feel like having my dinner in front of my favorite TV shows!", she continued.

It sounded to me like some disquieting energy had taken over in the room, so I asked her, "Do you remember anything happening in the room lately, anything that upset you, or any visit you might have had that occurred in the past month or so?"

She recalled that she had a meeting in her living room for committee members of her favorite charity, and they had discussed holding a fund raiser for a local animal shelter. She recalled that a couple of the attendees had been in disagreement over the arrangements, and that several heated discussions had taken place. But she explained that it all had been resolved by the end of the evening. However, she could not recall spending time in her living room involved in her creative projects since that event.....

To Think About...

It is important to carry out Sage and Smudge rituals in the common areas of your home on a regular basis. You may have people over to dinner, your children may have brought home their friends to study or to play; visitors may have come to spend time with you or a member of your family for a variety of reasons. The "common areas" are the parts of your home where you interact with your family members or roommates on a regular basis. Even sales representatives who knock on the door, repair or delivery service providers might on occasion be invited to enter the common areas of your home.

Sometimes you (or a family member) will watch something unpleasant, even frightening, on the television in one of the rooms in the common area of your home. A lot of violence is shown on a daily basis (even in the news!), and you or others who share this space may spend time with video games or movies that give rise to strong emotions. You may have disturbing telephone conversations in these rooms, or you and/or other members of your household may become involved in disagreements and arguments with one another. Even when you don't think anything could have happened to alter the energy balance in your environment, it sometimes does!

What you will be doing in a ritual of this nature is "re-claiming" your space and your sense of security and comfort, reminding the energies and spirits around you to protect, guard and support you in your life. You are letting the Universe (and your God) know that you are seeking help to maintain peace in your home.

The woman who is carrying out her Clearing Ritual at the beginning of this chapter offers an example of a "Re-Claiming Ritual" with several short "prayers" she uses while clearing her personal space of negativity. You might want to jot these affirmations down on a piece of paper or in your journal and use them (or similar ones) in your own Clearing and Re-Claiming rituals.

It's a good idea to keep a journal of your Sage and Smudge activities to record your thoughts before and after a ritual or ceremony. If this thought appeals to you, have your journal close by so you can write in it after you have finished clearing your space. (If you don't like to write in a journal, allow yourself a few moments to sit quietly in the room you have cleared after the ritual has been completed.)

Tips and Tools

Many people have a habit of doing a brief Clearing and Cleansing ritual every month at the time just before the New Moon, to clear the parts of their home of any negative vibrations. They often choose to use a Desert Sage Stick to drive out negative energy and influences. Some prefer to use either a White Sage Wand or loose White Sage leaves burned in a shell because of the sweeter aroma this herb gives off.

Whichever type of Sage you prefer is fine for the purpose of clearing the common areas of your home - usually the living room, kitchen, dining room, halls or a bathroom used by several people. Methods for using either type of sacred smoke herb are described below. If you are thinking about carrying out a Monthly Sage and Smudge Ritual with the objective of clearing out an "unpleasant" or uncomfortable feeling in one or more common areas in your home, here are some questions to consider:

- Think about how the space felt before you began to wonder whether negativity was present. Ask yourself: "Do I, or do other members of the household avoid spending time in this space?"
- See if you can define when the energy "shifted". Determine if you feel "tired" in that room now, or if you put off doing creative activities or spending time alone in the space.
- Do you feel the room is "dark", and do you find yourself turning on additional lights in the evening when you are in the room? Or do you pull back the drapes and open the shades or the windows to let in

more sunlight and air than usual during daylight hours?

If you are feeling "tired" or turning on more lights and opening shades and blinds to let in more sunlight, you may need to burn some Juniper in addition to the Sage. Sage and Juniper Wands are available, usually wrapped in two or more different, brightly-colored threads. Select colors that you like, and plan on having this wand for a while. It will be the one you use any time you feel that your environment needs a "pick-me-up" energy-wise!

If you find it is difficult to carry on a conversation in a particular room or area of your home, or it's hard to feel intimate with your loved ones, you might want to burn Cedar along with the Sage. You can find Sage and Cedar Wands as well, and may want to have both the Sage/Cedar and the Sage/Juniper Wands at home to use in the future for Clearing and Re-claiming rituals.

Before you start your Sage and Smudge ritual, look around the room or the area of your home that you are going to clear of negative energy. Look at the furniture and the decorations in the room. Spend a little time cleaning the room, dusting or vacuuming, or picking up, so the room is tidy before you begin.

If you (like Gail the example above) enjoy doing certain activities in this room, place something in the room that signifies the activity. You can place it on a table or other flat surface, in a chair or on a sofa you usually occupy while you are doing things you like to do in the room. If you feel that the negativity in the space has originated with a member of your household or as a result of some interaction between you and someone else, place a picture of the person on a table in the room before you start your ritual.

Sometimes people prefer to use loose White Sage leaves or a combination of sacred smoke herbs in this type of ritual. When using loose herbs place them in the shell (or container) in which you are going to burn them, and place the shell in a central location in the room on a heat resistant surface.

If you plan to use crushed Desert Sage, Cedar and/or Juniper to create your sacred smoke, it is a good idea to collect the whole herbs for the ritual, bring them into the room you are planning to clear and crush them together in your mortar with your pestle as part of the clearing ritual. In that case you can, as you prepare the herbs for the ritual, repeat your clearing affirmation or prayer three times before you place the crushed herbs in the container in which you will burn them.

When the herbs are ready to use, place the charcoal in the container you have chosen, light it and then sprinkle the smudge herbs on top. Wait until smoke is rising from the vessel. Waft the smudge up towards the ceiling with your feather or fan (or with your hand). Then move the smoke in the four directions (North, East, South and West) before you begin to clear the room and the furniture in it.

Be prepared to place more herbs in the container as needed during the clearing. As you are carrying out the Clearing and Re-claiming ritual, look at each part of the room, piece of furniture or decor. And be aware of your smudge to be sure that smoke continues to rise straight up from the container you are using during the ritual.

If the aromatic smoke should stop rising at any time, become very "thin", or move in the opposite direction of where you are standing as you are carrying out your ritual, wait to see if the smoke starts rising again if you stand still for a moment repeating your affirmation or prayer for the space. If it does not, return to your smudge vessel, add more herbs, or re-ignite as needed before you continue clearing the room.

Pay special attention to the area in the room where you were standing (or the objects you were clearing) when the smoke stopped rising or when you needed to go and add more herbs or re-ignite your sacred smoke. Always go back to where you were when you were "interrupted" and repeat your affirmation before you continue. This will ensure that you thoroughly clear the space. Continue your clearing ritual around the room once the smoke again rises towards the ceiling or if it moves in the direction of where you are standing.

If you are going to use a Sage and Smudge Wand, have a lighter and a small plate or bowl to carry with you as you smudge the room to catch any particles that may fall from the wand. (You don't want to spread any smoldering herb particles or ash on the carpet and furniture!)

If there is more than one door or entrance-way leading into the part of the common area you plan to clear, think about the direction you most commonly enter the room. If you feel that the disturbance came into the space with other people, think about how they entered the room, and start your clearing at that entrance.

As you begin your ritual, stand at the entrance-way you have chosen. This now becomes the "starting point" for your Sage and Smudge Re-Claiming Ritual. After you light your Sage wand, watch carefully as the herbs start to glow to see which direction the smoke rises and wafts out over the room.

If the smoke rises and moves to the right (counter-clockwise), you will carry out your clearing ritual walking to the right, around the room. If it rises and moves to the left (clockwise), you will carry out your ritual walking to the left around the room. If you can't determine which direction is indicated, move in a clockwise direction (to your left as you face into the room) as you carry out your ritual.

Carry the wand at the chest level, holding it out 8-12 inches from your body. Move slowly around the room as described at the beginning of this chapter, stopping to face into the middle of the room as you come to each corner. Clear any furniture as you clear the wall closest to where they stand. Furniture standing in the "middle" of the room can be cleared as you arrive at the mid-point of the third wall in the room.

Spend a few moments moving your wand around and above these pieces of furniture to make sure that any remaining unwelcome energy is detected. You will know if you find this kind of energy, because the smoke will "thin" or move in the opposite direction of the piece by which you are standing. This indicates an energy blockage.

If this happens, position yourself facing the piece of furniture, take a step back and move your wand from side to side in front of it (or above it) three times. Say: "Clear and remove any negative energy from this space. Bring blessings and peace into this room." Pause and wait until you see the smoke rising towards the ceiling once more before continuing on with your ritual. If the smudge does not rise, repeat once again. Repeat this up to three times, and if by then the sacred smoke still is not rising towards the ceiling, continue on with your clearing ritual. Make a note to yourself to return to this area and smudge the piece of furniture at another time.

Smudge all decorations, pictures and other wall fixtures as you clear the wall they hang on. Stop at each window, corner and doorway or entrance into the room, repeating your prayer or affirmation for the space. Spend a few extra moments clearing the furniture you usually occupy in the room, to make sure that they and the space around them are cleansed of all negativity.

If you have a picture in the room of someone with whom you want to clear your "relationship energy", spend a few moments making sure of the direction the smoke takes as you smudge around their picture. Wait until the smoke rises when your wand is held near the picture before continuing with the clearing ritual in the rest of the room.

When you have finished clearing your space, move towards the door where you began the ritual, and "usher out" any residual unwelcome influences, asking them to leave your home. You might say: "Clear and remove any negative energy from this room and from this home now. I call blessings of love, joy, comfort and well-being into this space and ask for protection from any negativity." Repeat your prayers and affirmation for the room three times. Then stand quietly near the entrance for a moment, looking into the room you have just cleared.

Breathe in and out the fragrance of the herbs you have used as you concentrate on the air entering and leaving your body. Usually a very simple prayer or affirmation (like the ones in the example at the beginning of the chapter) is sufficient to say as you finish the ritual, or say: "With this sacred smoke I clear this space of any negative energy. I ask all uninvited influences to leave this house now. I invite love, joy, comfort and peace to fill this space." Then take the wand either to the sink to douse the fire, or place it briefly in a glass or cup of water. Place the dampened wand in a safe place to dry. Return to the room you cleared, sit down and either record your thoughts, or simply relax quietly for a few minutes.

If you have used loose herbs to clear and heal the energy in your room(s), allow them to burn out on their own after you have finished your ritual. You can sit or stand quietly in the room for a short time after you have completed your ritual, thinking about it. Or, simply relax and feel the positive energy in the room. After the shell or container has cooled down, remove it, tip out the ashes and place your tools back in the place where you keep them in between your rituals. This type of ritual usually only takes a 5-10 minutes, and is well worth the time you spend on it!

Chapter 10

Clearing and Protecting Your Vehicle

The Sage and Juniper Wand he has chosen for his process this afternoon is about 8 inches long, and just a bit over an inch thick. He has selected a powerful tool for the Garage and Vehicle Clearing Ritual he is preparing to carry out. The wand is tightly wrapped with the red and yellow thread he chose to represent his focus this afternoon. He wants his garage to be a place where, in addition to parking his car, he can safely store his tools and some miscellaneous possessions. And he wants to protect his vehicle from harm! He is planning to give himself a kind of "extra insurance policy" with today's Sage and Smudge Clearing rituals.

He looks around in the dim light from the single window, observes the closed garage door, the storage cabinets and workbench along the side wall. He studies the many tools he has hung carefully in an easily accessible way on the wall above his workbench. He has swept out the garage in preparation for this ritual, and is ready now to get started.

He checks his pocket for the green cigarette lighter he likes to use - yes, it's right there. Then he walks over to one side of the closed garage door, holds his lighter to the Sage wand and watches as the flame begins to ignite the dry herbs. After a moment or two, he blows gently on the flames to encourage them to start smoldering inside the wand. He waits until a steady amount of smudge begins to rise from the wand. Now he is ready to begin.

Bending down to the floor, he holds the wand for a moment at the very bottom corner of his garage door. He says his Clearing words for the garage: "I call blessings of safety and positive energy into this space. Guard my possessions and my vehicle, and protect this space from any intrusion; negative energy and uninvited people are stopped from entering my garage. May this garage and all things in it be protected and may they bring benefit to my life!"

Satisfied that he has stated his intent for this Garage Clearing ritual, he stands up once again, and begins walking along the length of the garage door to the first corner of this space. In each corner he will repeat his Garage Clearing affirmation. Reaching this first corner, he looks along the garage wall with his cabinets, workbench and tools as he prepares to smudge them.

He starts walking along this wall, holding his Sage wand comfortably out from the midsection of his body. He keeps an eye on the smoke rising from the wand at each step, to make sure it goes straight up towards the roof of his garage. When he reaches the built-ins, he opens the front cabinet doors and moves the Sage and Juniper wand into each shelf opening, affirming out loud: "Clear all negative energy from this space. Protect my stuff. Bring benefit to my life in every way possible."

He repeats this affirmation as he clears his workbench and the tools hanging above it on the wall. And he repeats the affirmation as he opens and clears the shelves and drawers of his work and hobby space all along this wall of his garage.

At the second corner, he faces into the center of the garage, holds the wand out from his chest and repeats his affirmation for the space in general: "I call blessings of safety and positive energy into this space. Guard my possessions and my vehicle, and protect this space from any intrusion; negative energy and uninvited people are stopped from entering my garage. May this garage and all things in it be protected and may they bring benefit to my life!"

Then he quickly clears the remaining walls and the window, returns to the point at which he started his Garage Clearing. Standing still there for a moment, he watches the sacred smoke rising towards the roof. He feels confident that any unwelcome energy that may have accumulated there over the past few weeks has been cleared from the space.

He plans to continue this morning's ritual by clearing his car. He will use the same wand for that purpose so he leans it carefully against the cement wall near the garage door. Then using the handle on the inside of his garage door to lift it into place, he opens his garage to the world outside. His car is parked conveniently outside on the driveway and he walks towards it, ready to drive it into its now cleared parking space inside the garage.....

If you are fortunate enough to have your own personal vehicle - car, truck, SUV, motorcycle, motorbike, recreational vehicle, golf cart or dirt bike - it is most important to consider that this vehicle serves as your "protective shield" as you move through the streets, cities and journeys of your life. For that reason it is a good idea to consider carrying out regular Sage and Smudging rituals to clear and protect the vehicle from the various types of energy it (and you) may encounter out there in the world! Sage and Smudge rituals to clear and protect the vehicle fall into several categories:

1. Clearing the garage or parking space where your vehicle is to be parked when it is "at home".
2. Clearing the vehicle itself.
3. Clearing the part of the vehicle where you (and your loved ones) sit while inside (or on top of) it.

Part I
Clearing the garage (or parking space)

First, let's consider the home garage. When people buy or move into a house with a garage, it is not customary to ask the former residents whether or not they have ever been involved in an accident with their vehicles. And it is very unlikely you can find out whether or not they have experienced any of the whole variety of problems people can have with a personal or family vehicle! For that reason, if you move into a home with a garage it is best to assume that there have been problems of one kind or another connected to the vehicles driven/owned by the former residents of the home.

You will want to carry out a Sage and Smudge ritual in the garage before housing your own vehicle(s) in it! And you will want to keep your vehicle safe with your own "alternative insurance policy" during the time the vehicle - and the garage that houses it - is in your possession!

To Think About...

As a part of your home security considerations, you will want to test the mechanism by which the door to the garage is opened - including any keys that open the outer locks, changing the access codes on your garage door opener, testing the ease with which your garage door glides up and down, and opening, closing and locking any other doors leading into or out of the garage. Sometimes there is a garage door that leads directly into the residence. In that case, as you carry out your clearing process in the house, you will have smudged that door from inside to protect your home from any unwelcome "intrusion". Now it is appropriate to smudge this door from inside the garage.

Check to see if there are any windows or other openings both to the garage itself, and from the garage to the home. For instance: The hot water heater may be in the garage, with pipes leading into the house. The washer or dryer may be placed in the garage, and you may find an opening to the outside behind the dryer. Spend a little extra time smudging in these areas.

Look to see if there are storage cabinets or other types of designated work areas in the garage; pay special attention to them while you are smudging the space. When you have checked all of these things, look to see if there are indications on the floor of the garage that the vehicles of former owners have leaked or left other kinds of "souvenirs" there. If the garage floor is dusty or there is any kind of mess, clear it out, clean it up and sweep the floor before you start your Sage and Smudge clearing ritual.

Tips and Tools

Most people find it best to start a 2-part Garage and Vehicle Clearing ritual inside the garage with all of the doors and windows closed and secured. Start by clearing the garage itself. With the garage door closed, face towards the street and the driveway that leads into the garage.

Choose a White Sage Wand, a Sage and Juniper Wand or one comprised of White Sage and Cedar for this Clearing. You want to both clear the space in the garage itself and set protective boundaries with your ritual. (If you are using a Sage Wand you use for a variety of rituals, be sure to include a request for protection as a part of your Garage Clearing affirmation and blessing.)

At the left corner of the garage door, light your Sage wand with a lighter, remaining still until the Sage is smoking steadily and the smoke is rising towards the ceiling or the roof of the garage (if the interior is "unfinished"). This may take several minutes, and you may have to relight the wand more than once before you have a good, steady stream of smoke rising from it.

See whether or not the sacred smoke rises. If it seems to diffuse in all directions, wait until it does rise up, repeating words similar to the blessing or affirmation in the introduction to this chapter.

After the smoke begins to rise, bend down, hold the Sage wand at floor level. Move your wand up and along the left side of the garage door. Then, holding the wand comfortably at the level of your midsection, walk slowly along the entire garage door. As you walk, say or chant:

"Protect, protect, clear this space of any negative energy and protect all that is kept in this garage. Protect the vehicles that will be in this space, and guard against intrusion." Repeat these phrases when you reach the right side of the garage door.

At the right edge of the garage door, stand still for a few moments and watch to see the direction of the movement of the smoke from your Sage wand. It should preferably rise up towards the roof or ceiling of your structure, or move gently in the direction of the interior of the garage. If it does not, repeat your affirmation for the Garage Clearing, moving the wand along the length of the right edge of the garage door opening from floor to top. Then stand still again for a moment.

(Since a garage door is seldom "air tight" it is possible that you will not be able to know for sure if wind or other factors affect the movement of the Smudge as you clear the garage door and its opening. It is quite appropriate to continue with the Garage Clearing after you have repeated your affirmation three times - even if the smudge is not moving in the manner described in this paragraph.)

Continue your Sage and Smudge ritual along the remaining part of the entrance wall to the first corner of the space. At the corner turn to face into your garage. Look towards cupboards, shelves, other built-in space or work and storage areas along the walls in your garage. Think about how you will use the space in this area of your garage. These things in mind, walk slowly around the walls of the garage, clearing the space ahead of you as you move forward.

Hold the wand comfortably in your left hand at a level between your waist and your chest as you walk, stopping to smudge anything placed or stored along the walls. Keep observing the direction the smudge rises into the air, and if it should sink towards the floor or drift out into the center of the garage, stop for a moment and repeat your affirmation for the space. Continue when the smoke rises above you once again.

If there are specific areas of the garage intended for storage, work or hobbies, stop in front of these, face them (open any doors or drawers) and smudge these spaces thoroughly. Proceed from the floor to top of these interior structures. Think about how you or your family members will use this space, and if you wish, you can say a special affirmation for any of these areas as you clear them.

As you walk around your garage clearing your space, stop to repeat your "chant" at all doorways, windows and other openings either into the home or to the outside. Continue in this manner until you return to the starting point of your Garage Clearing ritual.

When you have completed your clearing around the interior walls, walk to the middle of the floor of your garage. Holding your Sage wand in both hands, watch the sacred smoke rise above you. Breathe in the aroma of the herbs three times.

Imagine your vehicle(s) in the space, the things that belong to you in their specific places in the garage. Then repeat the Clearing and Blessing affirmation for your garage as you claim the entire space of the garage for the your own purpose. When you are done, leave using either the entry door to your home from inside the garage, or the garage door that you will use most often coming and going to your parked car inside.

If there is no doorway between the home and the garage, exit the garage in the way you normally will use when going from your vehicle into your home. Carry the still smoldering Sage wand with you all the way into your home, and extinguish it behind closed doors inside your home. This pulls the energy of your Garage Clearing ritual with you along the pathway you will follow between your garage and your house and ensures safety along that route as well.

Part II
Clearing a Vehicle

Whether you have a garage (or other type of specified parking space on your property), or you park your vehicle on a public street, in a public or private parking lot or on the road in front of your home, you will want to smudge the interior of your vehicle on a regular basis to disperse any negative energy that may attach to your vehicle. It is also a good idea to smudge on a regular basis if you regularly park your vehicle in a parking facility or on the street while you work or run your errands. It is wise to maintain a "safe and protected space" surrounding your vehicle at all times whether it is "at home" or out in the world!

Let's take a look at a Sage and Smudge ritual to clear a vehicle:

.....His car now parked inside the garage, he returns to the place where he rested his Sage and Juniper wand against the wall. He checks to see that it is still smudging, then he once again closes the garage door, securing the space from any outside influences. He turns to pick up the wand and approaches his car. He has cleared it many times before - it's something he likes to do at least once a month at the time of the First Quarter Moon.

He walks around to the front of the car and facing it he begins his Sage and Smudge Vehicle Clearing ritual. Moving the Sage and Juniper wand to his left hand, he repeats his usual blessing for the vehicle: "Safety surrounds you. You are protected from any harm or danger." He bends slightly, and moves the smoldering wand around each of the front lights, the fender, the hood and the front windshield. Then he stands up and watches the direction the sacred smoke is moving. Good! Straight up into the space above the car.

He moves clockwise around the vehicle, clearing first one side, then the back, and then the other side. He pauses for a brief moment at each side of his vehicle as he clears them, repeating his affirmation for safety and protection. Then, back at the front of his vehicle, he walks to the driver's side of the car, opens the door, sits down in the driver's seat and places the handle of his Sage wand in a cup holder in the console between his seat and the front passenger seat.

Placing both hands on the steering wheel, he breathes deeply three times, inhaling then exhaling the scent of the sacred smoke. He says: "All who travel in this vehicle are protected. It is safe to ride and be in this vehicle. When I drive this vehicle, my mind is clear, I am aware of the road and all others traveling on it. I am careful of the laws, quick of thought and reflex." Finally, he says: "Protect me, and protect my journey through life!"

Carefully picking up the Sage Wand from the cup-holder, he steps out of his vehicle, closes the front door, and stands still for a moment watching the smoke rise thickly into the air above his car. He affirms: "All is well in my world!" and walks over to the box of sand he keeps in a corner of his garage. He points the top of his wand down and pushes it into the sand, making sure that it is buried more than halfway so the embers will be extinguished. He will return to his garage later this evening. Then he will lift out the wand, shake out any of the grains of sand from the leaves and twigs, and place the wand in the drawer where he keeps it in between his regular clearings.

To Think About...

It is always easier to carry out a Sage and Smudge ritual on a vehicle in an enclosed garage. So, when you feel it is necessary to smudge your vehicle, the best place to do so is in your garage. Here are some examples of times when it is appropriate to Sage and Smudge your vehicle:

- When you purchase a new vehicle.
- When an incident has occurred that has damaged the vehicle.
- When/if a ticket has been placed on your car (parking violation is the most common).
- When/if a ticket has been issued (moving violation is the most common).

- When the vehicle has been involved in an accident, or had extensive repair.
- When the vehicle has been in the hands of a mechanic for service or repair.
- When the vehicle has been driven by someone other than yourself and your family members (with or without your permission).

Personal circumstances may also indicate - on a spiritual or esoteric level - it is time to smudge your vehicle. Examples of these are:

- If you have accepted a new job (or promotion), and will be traveling to a new destination for work on a regular basis.
- If you have met a new person who is becoming a significant relationship for you and they begin to be with you in the vehicle on a regular basis (or you begin driving to see and spend time with them on a regular basis).
- If a new baby arrives.
- If a new person moves into your life (and your residence), and they will regularly be with you in the vehicle (or drive the vehicle).
- If someone who drove the vehicle regularly is no longer living with you, or a significant relationship has come to an end.
- If you "hit" an animal or drive over something "dead" on the road.
- If there has been a "near miss" type of situation on the drive to or from a regular destination, where an

accident could have happened, or a ticket could have been issued.

- In preparation for a longer trip than usual in the vehicle - like a vacation or a business trip where you will be gone from your home more than one night.
- If your vehicle has been parked in a public parking facility (at the airport, for instance) for more than 24 hours.

Note: Smudge your vehicle if for any reason you feel "uncomfortable" driving or riding in it, or if others have driven it without your permission. Always carry out a Sage and Smudge ritual in your vehicle if you have an "uncomfortable feeling" after transporting other people or goods in it!

Tips and Tools

If it is convenient for you to do so, it is a good idea to smudge the vehicle both around the outside, and on the inside (or "on top" of the seat of a motorcycle, for example; see below). You can use a Sage wand for this purpose as described in the introduction to this section of the chapter. Loose White Sage leaves are also a popular selection for clearing most vehicles.

For a Vehicle Clearing ritual using loose herbs or leaves of White Sage, you will need a vessel in which to place them, and a feather or fan of some kind to move the smoke in the direction you choose during the ritual. People often place a selection of loose herbs or White Sage leaves in a shell, and I also recommend a thick ceramic bowl or a vessel of some other material that will contain the heat.

When selecting a vessel to use for your Sage and Smudge Vehicle Clearing rituals, it is a good idea to consider in advance whether or not it will become too hot to hold in one hand, or to rest on the palm of your hand during a 5-10 minute ritual. If it is going to become too hot to hold comfortably, then you will need to protect your hand from being burned. A hot pad, thick cloth or glove may be useful to protect your hand from harm.

Before you begin the ritual, gather your Sage leaves, shell or vessel, thick protective cloth or glove, a fan or feather, and a lighter or matches. Take them into your garage or to your vehicle. Unlock the car doors so you can open them readily as you proceed.

If you are clearing your vehicle in your garage, you can clear both inside and outside the vehicle easily. If you do not have a private garage, think about whether you plan to smudge the outside of your vehicle, or if you only plan to smudge the inside. It may be inconvenient to smudge the outside of the vehicle if it is in a parking area designated for many people to use, one which is in view of your neighbors. It may also be inconvenient (or draw unwanted attention) to smudge outside your vehicle if you park it on the street. In that case, plan to do your ritual inside the vehicle.

Place at least three (or multiples of three) leaves of White Sage in the shell or other ritual vessel. (Three is the number associated with Mercury - and Mercury symbolizes movement, transportation and "communication". Therefore three leaves of White Sage or three pieces of whole herbs (or multiples of three pieces or leaves) are the appropriate selection for a Vehicle Clearing ritual using loose herbs.) Light the leaves individually and allow them to flare up for a moment before shaking them lightly or blowing on them gently to cause them to "smoke" and form the smudge you need for the ritual.

If you are able to do this ritual in your garage or in a private place, hold the shell with the burning smudge in your left hand out from your body at about waist level. You may have to light some of the leaves several times before you are ready to begin. Take your feather or fan in your right hand and approach the front of your vehicle. Facing the front of the vehicle, you might say: "Safety surrounds you and you are protected from any harm or danger." Fan the rising smudge in the direction of each of the front lights, the fender, the hood and the windshield.

Then, moving clockwise around the vehicle, approach the passenger door and say: "All who travel in this vehicle are protected. It is safe to ride and be in this vehicle". Fan the smudge along the passenger side of the vehicle, paying special attention to any mirrors on that side of the vehicle, the door opening itself, and the passenger windows along that side of the vehicle.

As you move towards the back of the vehicle, smudge any additional passenger door and window, then stop for a moment at the back and say, "Where you park, where you stop, where you move ahead of others, you are visible to them, and they are careful of your space. This vehicle is protected from all harm."

Then continue along the driver's side, fanning the smudge towards the vehicle. Pause at the driver's door, and as you fan the smudge towards the opening, say, "May I be clear of mind as I drive this vehicle, aware of the road and all the other energies (drivers, vehicles, pedestrians and other creatures) traveling on it, careful of the laws governing the movement of this vehicle along the roads of life, quick of thought and reflex. Help me to see clearly and drive safely. Protect me while I drive this vehicle. Protect this vehicle from harm." (Make sure to smudge any exterior mirror and the driver's window as well.)

Now, open the door on the driver's side of the vehicle and place the shell (or other vessel with the Sage smoking in it) on the floor of the car. Say, "When I drive, let me see the road clearly, and help me to be mindful of the rules governing the roads. I am protected from anything that could harm me. I am respectful of all life and mean no harm to any other. Protect me, and protect my journey through life!"

Move the shell to the floor in front of the passenger seat. "Protect all who sit beside me." Then, going around to the passenger side of the vehicle, open the door and lift out the shell. Open the back door of the vehicle - if there is a back door - and place the shell on the floor of the back seat. (Otherwise simply reach the shell over to the floor in the back seat of the vehicle.) Say: "Protect all who accompany me in this vehicle."

Now remove the shell from the back seat floor, take it and walk around to the back of your vehicle and open the trunk. Place the shell and the smoking sage leaves in the trunk. With the trunk open, say: "All that is placed in this space is protected from harm. This space is protected. No

one may remove anything from this space without my permission."

Lift the shell out of the trunk, step to one side of the vehicle and, with all of the doors and trunk open, affirm: "This vehicle is now safe and protected from all negative energy!" Then close the doors and the trunk, and your ritual is complete.

If you wish, you can allow the loose Sage leaves or herbs to burn until they stop after completing your Sage and Smudge ritual. Otherwise, you can tip out the smudge herbs into some sand or earth. After the embers are out, you can bury the ash and remaining herbs in the earth. Do not "wash" your ritual shell (or vessel) but put it in a safe place until you use it again.

If you are unable to (or it is very inconvenient to) smudge the exterior of the vehicle, or you want to take only a short time for your ritual, then simply smudge the interior of the vehicle. In that case use three small dry leaves of Sage, take a shell and a small fan or feather with you into the car. Sit inside the vehicle (in the driver's seat), light each leaf.

When smoke is rising from the smudge vessel, hold it in your left hand, and, fanning the smoke around you in the vehicle with your fan or feather, move it in the direction of the front and side windows of the vehicle from your seat, saying, "Safety surrounds my vehicle; it is protected from any harm or danger. When I drive I see clearly and my mind is clear, focused on my journey. I am aware of the road and the other energies traveling on it and careful of the laws governing the movement of the vehicle. I think quickly and my reflexes are good. Protect this vehicle. I am respectful of all life and mean no harm to any other. Protect me and my journey through life."

Then place the shell beside you on the passenger seat and say: "Protect all who sit beside me, and all who accompany me in this vehicle. All that is placed in the space inside this vehicle is protected from harm." Complete your Sage and Smudge ritual by placing the shell on the floor of the vehicle (front seat, back seat or trunk) and allowing the Sage leaves to finish smudging on their own.

After completing any Sage and Smudge ritual in your vehicle, open the doors or windows and the trunk to allow some of the smudge and the intense scent from the burning herbs to escape into the air outside. As the essence of the energy of your ritual disperses into the air outside, it will enfold your vehicle, protecting the outside of it as well.

There will be a scent of Sage in the vehicle for some time after a ritual. If this bothers you or any of your passengers, driving with the windows open for a day or so may be necessary. You may want to place/hang one of the special automobile deodorizers inside to lessen the intensity of the herbs you have burned. Some people have success placing a little baking soda in the ashtrays in the back seats and keeping them open to absorb the scent. You could also place a salt shaker with baking soda in it on the floor of the back seat. Or, if you like, you can sprinkle baking soda over the carpet on the floor of the vehicle, and vacuum up the powder after an hour or two. Of course, you can carry out a Vehicle Clearing ritual using the "casting" technique if an aromatic sacred smoke one is not possible.

PART III
BICYCLES, MOTORBIKES OR MOPEDS

If you are carrying out a Sage and Smudge ritual for a bicycle, motorbike or moped, you can either use a Sage Wand for your ritual, or loose Sage leaves placed in a shell. Take care to use a feather to fan the smoke in the direction of your vehicle as you do the ritual. (Feathers symbolize speed and movement through the air, and are a good representation of the energy of your vehicle.)

Start by facing the front of the vehicle, and walk around it in a clockwise direction as you carry out your Sage and Smudge ritual. Carry the smoldering Sage wand (or the shell with smoking Sage leaves) alongside your vehicle, making sure to smudge the whole thing. Out loud, say: "Safety surrounds this vehicle and its travels on the highways and byways of life. When I drive this vehicle my mind is clear, I am aware of the road and the other energies traveling on it. I am mindful of the laws governing all movement on the roads. I think quickly and I have good reflexes when needed. I am respectful of all life and intend no harm to any other. Protect me and my journey through life, and protect my vehicle. Protect all that is placed in (or on) this vehicle."

Complete your Sage and Smudge ritual by placing the shell on the ground in front of the vehicle and allowing the herbs to burn out by themselves. If you are using a Sage wand, place the smoking end of the wand in a basin of sand you have placed near the vehicle at the start of the ritual. Leave the wand in the sand for at least 15 minutes, and check to see that the embers have indeed gone out before putting it back where you keep your Sage and Smudge tools when you are not using them.

Chapter 11

Sage and Smudge Personal Possessions

Holding the Sage and Juniper wand in her left hand, she lifts the flame at the end of her long, wooden match to the tip of the wand. She watches as the White Sage leaves begin to burn. The flame licks the ends of the Juniper twigs as well and she lets the dancing fire burn for half a minute to make sure that the Sage and Juniper wand will continue smudging when she is ready to proceed with her clearing ritual. Then she blows gently towards the end of her wand, observing the glow that forms inside it as the flame subsides. Smudge rises thickly into the air, and she breathes in the scent of the "woody essence" now filling the space. Already she feels more relaxed, less tense, her emotions are evening out.

The boxes of books arrived yesterday. She has intense feelings of sadness and loss as she opens the boxes and looks over the contents. Her dear friend had left these treasures to her when he gave instructions about what to do with his things after he was gone. Each book is a reminder of the many conversations and thoughts they had shared with one another. And she wants to enjoy reading and studying them in the future, to be reminded only of the good times spent in conversation and friendship - not the sadness and emptiness she now feels as she touches them.

She settles down on the floor in front of the bookcase that will be "home" to the collection. Holding the wand now in her dominant hand, she picks up one of the books with her left hand in order to smudge it thoroughly before placing it on a shelf. She moves the wand with the thickly rising sacred smoke around the front, back and sides of the book saying: "Clear any negative or sad energy from this book." Then she places this first book on the shelf and reaches for the next one from the box beside her. She will repeat this clearing with each book in the collection.

Half an hour later, she looks at the empty boxes that had once held the books now neatly arranged in their new place on the shelves of her bookcase. She stretches, breathes deeply of the scent of Sage and Smudge for a moment, looking at the books in front of her. She turns and walks over to the now empty boxes. Moving her Sage wand over them, she says: "Clear any negative energy from these boxes."

She sets down the handle end of her Sage wand in a coffee mug she uses as a "holder" during rituals that have several parts to them. Then she places the mug on the round glass-topped table in one corner of her study, watching the thick smoke still rising from the wand for a moment. She turns and picks up the boxes to move them to the garage where they will be stored until she can take them to be recycled in a week or two.

Returning to her study after clearing away the packing material, she goes over to the still smoking wand, picks it up and walks to the front of her bookcase. She holds the wand once again in her right hand and moves it from side to side the whole height of the filled shelves in front of her (from floor to top), saying: "These books are now cleared of all negative or sad energy. I claim them as my own, as my friend wished. Only positive energy, positive memories, will surround these books. Everything on these shelves serves to benefit me in the future!"

She stands still in front of and facing the bookcase when she has finished, watching the smoke rise towards the ceiling of the room. She will always remember her friend with great fondness and gratitude, and now she will be able to enjoy reading and having this collection without any sad overtones. She walks at a moderate pace around the walls of her study, observing the rising smudge from her Sage and Juniper Wand. At the entrance to the room, she stops and says: "This room is filled with positive energy. Everything in this room serves to benefit my life and my purpose. I am thankful for the blessings I have received. Bless the spirit of my friend, and bless me."

She walks then to the garage once more, carrying the Sage and Smudge wand with her down the hallway. Entering the garage through the door that connects it with the rest of her home, she walks over to a container filled with sand she has placed in a corner of the garage space. She points the top of her wand down, and pushes it easily into the sand, burying it about to a point at least an inch below where she had observed the embers burning inside the wand. She turns the wand a couple of times, then stands up to see if any smoke is rising. No? Good. She will come back in half an hour or so, and remove the wand from the container, check to be sure it is cool to the touch. Then she will tap out any grains of sand, dip it in a mug filled with water, and stand it up to dry until the next time she needs to use it.

It's really wonderful when we receive a gift we like, or one that we can treasure - like the one received by the woman in the introduction. But that is not always the case! Have you ever looked at a gift that you received from someone and thought, "I wonder why they thought this was something I would like...?" or, "This is really not my taste. I'll put it away and only take it out when Aunt Betty comes to visit." or, "I'll never wear the color, but I can't throw the sweater away, because that would make him feel bad..."

Sometimes when we receive things from the people in our lives, we can feel obliged to keep these items - even if we have no use for them, or do not like them. We might not want to "hurt their feelings" by letting them know we don't need, like or want something they have given us. Sometimes, even when we are given something we do like, the gift may be from someone with whom we have unresolved issues of one kind or another. So, we may not feel like using the item, wearing the clothes, or enjoying the gift! In some instances, every time we look at this item, we are reminded of the "giver", and the issues we have with them.

At one time or another you may have received a "gift" from someone who was trying to manipulate you, someone who gives presents while at the same time expecting you to do something for them that you really would not choose to do - if you were given the choice! You may have felt obliged to help them out, simply because they have been so "generous".

Occasionally we are given something reminiscent of some past time in our lives. If pleasant memories are associated with these things, it can be fun to use them and share them with others. However, sometimes we receive things that recall sad or difficult times in our lives. When that happens, it may be difficult to use or even look at the things we have been given.

For example, Jeffrey received his father's engagement and wedding ring from his mother after his father had passed away. He did not want to wear them, and really did not know what to do with them. So he put them in the top drawer of the chest in his bedroom. Every time he opened that drawer to take something out he would see the little box with the rings, and feel guilty about not appreciating the gift his mother had given him - and sad about the loss of his father.

In another case, Sherri's father had died when she was very young. Her mother had not remarried, and Sherri had no siblings. When her mother died of cancer (Sherri was just 22 at the time) she became responsible for clearing out her mother's home and deciding what to keep and what to sell or give away. Overcome with the feeling of loneliness and depression, she was unable to look at the things that had been part of her mother's life and make any decision about what to do with them.

Ultimately she had everything but her mother's personal clothing (which she gave to a charity) moved into storage. Years later when Sherri was moving to another city because of a job opportunity, she decided to move her mother's things with her because she would have room in her new home for them. She couldn't justify keeping the things in storage any longer.

After the move, Sherri did unpack the boxes of things her mother had left. And she placed many of the items among her own things in her new home. But time after time, when she looked at her mother's things or used them, she would feel an overwhelming sense of loss and sadness that her mother was not there to be a part of her life.

One day, around Thanksgiving time, as she was polishing the silver to use for her Thanksgiving Dinner, she broke down completely, filled with regret, even guilt about the past. After that event, many of the lovely things that reminded her of the loss of her mother were once again packed away in boxes, and placed in the garage.

And then there is Linda, who had a very difficult childhood, and blamed her father for it. He and her mother divorced when Linda was in her early teens. Following the divorce, her father moved to another state, stopped providing any financial support, basically abandoning them. She didn't see him or hear from him for more than ten years. Then she started receiving letters from him, and they eventually reestablished some contact with one another - but on a very limited basis.

After her marriage and the birth of her first child, her father (who is doing very well financially) started sending extremely expensive presents to his grandson. Linda is very uncomfortable about the whole situation. Each time a gift arrives, she is reminded of the emotional conflict she experienced during the years her father was absent from her life, and the many hardships she and her mother faced following the divorce of her parents.

To think about...

Objects are surrounded by their own energy fields. When people touch objects, especially when there is an "emotional charge" surrounding the interchange of energy between the person and the object, some of the energy in the aura of the person "touching" enters the energy field surrounding the object "being touched".

Have you ever noticed that as you are browsing in a bookstore, or walking through a department store, that you are able to pass by many books or items, yet you are drawn to look at a few specific titles, or to examine a particular piece of clothing? If you touch something, it is probably because you find the item interesting. You want to know how it feels, or you are curious to find out more about it. For some reason, your energy field and that of the object are "drawn" to one another.

This "energy exchange", if you will, is what makes you feel that you would like to own something you see (or not own it, as the case may be). And whether you do buy the book, or buy the sweater you have been touching, you have in a way "felt a powerful connection" with the item. You give some of your energy (in the form of a desire to own it) to that object, and receive some from it in exchange! You feel some "pleasure" at the energy exchange and wish to continue to have access to this energy source in the future.

The interesting thing about these invisible "energy fields" is that every time someone touches an object, a little of the energy exchange that has taken place (even in a very brief exchange) allows each party - the individual and the object - to retain some of the other's "qualities". When you touch an object that has been handled, examined, desired or purchased by some other person, you come in contact with the other person's energy as well as the energy of the object. And the longer an object is in someone's possession, and the more that person "enjoys" the object, uses it, touches it, wears it, looks at it, etc., the more of that person's energy is transferred to the energy field surrounding the object!

When the people who have previously handled (or purchased) an item they give you have a "positive" relationship with you, you will feel some of this positive energy in the object you receive. When the people who have previously handled (or purchased) an item they give you have a "negative" relationship with you, you are likely to feel that energy as well. You will feel it when you hold, touch or even look at the object you have received. Your intuitive perception of the gift's (or object's) energy field will often determine whether you like what you have received, or not!

It is possible that you really dislike certain things that you receive from others. But what if you simply don't like the energy of the person who has given you the present? What if you don't feel comfortable with the emotions and feelings that are aroused by the memories or thoughts that come to mind when you are given something? These thoughts and feelings somehow become associated with an article or object you receive, and may cause you to wonder whether or not to keep the items - whether or not you like them!

If, on the other hand, you receive something that has belonged to someone you really cared for, their energy - associated with the object you have been given - may feel comforting. It is likely to remind you of all of the good times you shared with one another. Your feelings about such gifts and heirlooms are likely to reflect your feelings about the person who had them in their possession before you received them. (This is especially likely to happen when you receive things that have belonged to someone else for a long time.)

Tips and Tools

Prepare for your Sage and Smudge Clearing of objects, items or gifts by placing it/them on a table in front of you. Place a chair at the table, in "front" of the item you want to smudge. If you have received a very large object (such as a piece of furniture, a work of art or equipment of some kind) you cannot place on a table, place a chair in front of the object and refer to the description of how to do a clearing of larger items below.

If the object on the table can be lifted with one hand, you can use a Sage wand or stick for your clearing. But if the object requires you to use both hands to lift it, you may want to burn loose herbs in a shell or other heat-tolerant vessel for your sacred smoke ritual.

Consider using a combination of herbs to clear the "energy field" of objects. Cedar is especially good for clearing negative emotions. Mugwort will ensure the speedy removal of negative energy (and it will help you to be really clear about your own feelings in relation to the object). Juniper is considered excellent for purification and protection purposes. Or you might want to include some Mugwort with your Sage and Smudge herbs, as it is helpful for setting boundaries. (If you are aware that you have an issue with setting boundaries between yourself and whomever gave you the object or gift, you might benefit from burning this herb during your clearing ritual.)

Begin your Sage and Smudge clearing ritual sitting in the chair and facing the object. If the object can easily be placed on a table, sit down in front if it, and light the smudge you have selected for your clearing ritual. Hold your smudge stick or wand between you and the object in your dominant hand. If you are smudging with herbs in a shell or bowl, place the vessel on the table between yourself and the object on the table.

When the smoke is rising thickly from your wand or your container, gently blow the smoke in the direction of the object, to surround it with aromatic smoke. Turn the object so that you can see another side of it and gently blow the smoke towards the object once again. Continue in this manner until all sides of the object have been smudged. Then lift the article up in the air, and either pass your smudge wand under it, or move it four times through the sacred smoke rising from your smudge vessel.

A very simple statement is all that is needed for clearing an object of unwanted energy: "Cleanse, clear and remove all negative energy from this object." Repeat the phrase each time as you smudge the sides of the object, and as you move it through the smoke to smudge the bottom of it. (The top is smudged four times as you blow the smoke towards the object, as you clear each of the four sides.)

Place the object once again on the table again, and affirm: "This object is now cleared of all negative energy. I claim this object as my own. Only positive energy will surround this object. This object serves to benefit me in the future!"

You may now walk away from the object. Allow any remaining smudge herbs to burn themselves out in your smudge vessel. Or, if you have used a Sage Wand or Sage Stick, you can put it out at this point, after saying the "claiming" affirmation. (Use either water or earth to put out the burning Sage wand - whichever you prefer.)

If you need to clear a large object (one you need two hands to lift, for example), lift it up on the table and position it before you start. Move any chairs out from under the table, so you can easily walk around the object as you are carrying out your Sage and Smudge Clearing ritual. It is most convenient to use a Sage wand or stick for this type of clearing.

Start your Sage and Smudge Clearing by lighting the Sage wand you have chosen for this type of ritual. Wait until a thick smudge is rising from the wand, and then stand and approach the object from the front, gently blowing the smoke towards the "front" of the object. Walk around your table, and smudge each side of the object thoroughly, repeating at each side, "Cleanse, clear and remove all negative energy from this object." In order to smudge the bottom of the object, extend your Sage wand under the table and imagine yourself clearing the underside of the object. Or you can visualize the bottom of the object, and gently blow smoke in the direction of the object four times.

Repeat the affirmation for clearing negative energy. (If the object is going to be placed somewhere in your home, you can now smudge the space where you will place it, before moving the object from the table to it's new location.) Wait for a few moments, then put out your Sage wand in either water or earth, saying: "This object is now cleared of all negative energy. I claim this object as my own. Only positive energy will surround this object. This object serves to benefit me in the future!"

If you are going to Sage and Smudge a very large object (one you cannot readily lift and place on a table) and you are going to use a shell or a bowl for your Sage and Smudge clearing process, place the herbs in the container and light them as you normally do. Place a brick or some other heat-resistant material in front of the object on which to place your smudge vessel during the Sage and Smudge clearing. As soon as the herbs are creating a thick smoke, gently blow the smoke in the direction of the object.

You can either carry your smudge vessel with you (carefully, so you don't burn your hand) and walk around the object, stopping to blow the smoke towards the object from the four "sides", repeating the affirmation in the manner mentioned above. Or, you can combine placing a smudge container in "front" of the object and carrying a lighted smudge wand with you around the other sides of it. Repeat the affirmation: "Cleanse, clear and remove all negative energy from this object.", at each side of the heavy piece you are smudging. (This worked well for someone who had been given a washer and dryer).

After you have circled the heavy object, allow the herbs in the smudge vessel in front of the object to burn out, then say: "This object is now cleared of all negative energy. I claim this object as my own. Only positive energy will surround this object. This object serves to benefit me in the future!"

On occasion, when people have performed Sage and Smudge Clearings of objects, they find that they feel very differently about the object when the negative energy has been removed. They may still not "like" the gift/object they have received, but then they know for sure it is a question of their own "taste" in the matter. They know that their thoughts and emotions are not being influenced by negative energy associated with the item or their relationship with the person who gave it to them. Sometimes people find that they really like, need and will enjoy using or wearing the object/gift/item they have received following the Sage and Smudge Clearing ritual.

Either way, when you make a decision about using or keeping something you have received from someone else after carrying out your Sage and Smudge Clearing of the object, you will be able to make that choice based on your own decision. You are no longer influenced by the energy you "sense" surrounding the item!

Chapter 12

Personal Sage and Smudge Rituals

Picking up her Sage and Smudge journal, she opens to the section devoted to her personal rituals. Today has been very difficult, and on her way home from work she has decided that a Sage and Smudge Personal Clearing ritual is the only thing that will help her clear herself of the negativity she feels all around. She knows the difficult happenings of the day are impacting her on psychological, mental and emotional levels - and she wants to clear her "spirit essence" before the negativity can manifest physical symptoms. Today she was notified that she and more than 135 other employees will no longer have their jobs with their company. She has worked there for more than 6 years, and many of those who were given notice today are people she knows well, works with on a daily basis and really cares about.

Just thinking about it again fills her with both sadness and fear about the future. Will I find another job? So many others in my field are already looking for work. There is so much competition for every job that might become available! How will I manage my finances without the income I have counted on? How will I pay my debts - for the car and my credit cards? What about rent? Am I going to have to move?

What if I can't find work here, and I have to relocate? What will my parents think? What will my friends think? What?.... How? .... Why me?....

Sitting at her desk in the bedroom, many questions come to mind as she writes in her journal. She always makes notes about her frame of mind before doing a Personal Sage and Smudge ritual. And as she lists her questions, she attempts to write down her fears and really get in touch with the emotions that come up from inside. She gives herself permission to cry - for herself and all of the other good people she knows who are going through a similar experience today.

Then she makes an outline of the Personal Clearing she will carry out. She jots down a few prayers and affirmations on 3" x 5" cards to hold and read aloud as she carries out the ritual she is planning. She takes off the clothes and shoes she has been wearing this day, hangs her suit up on a hangar to take to the cleaners, which she hangs on the doorknob of her bedroom door. She puts the rest of what she was wearing today in the washing machine right away. She will not wear the garments again until they are clean and fresh - the energy of today's experiences washed all away!

She places her shoes in the middle of the floor at the end of her bed, along with her handbag - now open - and goes to fetch the Sage wand she uses for her personal clearings. She keeps it in the drawer of her nightstand, along with her lighter and a little red plate she uses to catch any falling ash or burning Sage particles during a ritual. She places the red plate in an open area of her floor, and stands a little to one side of it and lights her sage wand. Holding it in her right hand, she has to try lighting it several times before the embers begin to glow. Finally the smoke starts rising from the wand. She waits a few moments, standing there, watching the smoke rise, then fall, then rise again towards the ceiling.

Carefully she bends down and places the wand on the red plate. She waits again to see that the sacred smoke continues to rise from the wand on the plate at her feet. Then holding a yellow 3" x 5" card with her first prayer written on it, she says out loud as a prayer: "Please help me to overcome my fear and uncertainty. Help me to find healing from the sadness and fear that surrounds me. Help me to find the courage and the strength to get through the coming weeks, to be able to encourage my friends and co-workers, and to handle my responsibilities and the challenges that I meet. Help me to learn from this experience, help me to trust that this lesson is necessary. I want to understand what my spirit needs to learn from this experience."

Then she steps forward to stand above the smoke still rising from the wand. As it rises around her, surrounding her body and her aura, she stands still, breathing in the aromatic scent of the burning herbs. She begins to feel a calm settle over her wounded spirit. She affirms: "God loves me, and has a plan for me and for my life. I trust in his love and support. I am safe and protected. My life is of value. I am of value. I am loved." Then she steps forward once again, and allows the smudge to clear her back. Closing her eyes, she asks that she be protected even from the things that happen that she is not aware of. She asks that no harm come to her and that she find the help, support and encouragement she needs to go forward.

Finally she turns around to look at the wand on the red plate behind her on the floor. She bends down and picks up the wand, and walks to the suit hanging on the doorknob of her room. Carefully she moves the wand up and down, watching the smoke as it touches each part of this suit. "Clear any negative energy from this suit. Erase the energy of the things that happened today while I was wearing this garment. When I wear it again, may I feel confident and certain."

She turns around once again, and walks over to the shoes at the end of her bed. Bending down, she lifts the shoes in one hand, and moves the smudging Sage wand under them, saying "Clear any negative impressions and energy from these shoes. May they carry no energy from the experiences of today. May they carry me forward in my life as they have in the past. May I walk confidently towards my future! I will walk forward into the future, knowing that I will be safe, secure and protected. I am confident that my future is already being prepared for me."

Standing straight again, she holds her Sage wand out from her heart, and repeats her prayer for Personal Clearing: "God loves me, and has a plan for me and for my life. I trust in his love and support. I am safe and protected. My life is of value. I am of value. I am loved. I know that I am on my way into my future!"

She stands still for a few moments, feeling a sense of peace surround her. And then she goes towards her bathroom, douses the wand in running water from the faucet for a moment or two, places it on her red plate to one side of the sink to dry, and turns on the shower. She will complete her ritual by taking a shower and putting on fresh clothes. When she is done with that, she will sit at her desk once more and write down the thoughts that occurred to her while she was praying and carrying out the Personal Clearing. Later this evening, she will light a little crushed Sage, Mugwort and Rosemary in the earthenware container she has for such purposes on the nightstand beside her bed.

Have you ever spent time talking to someone and, as you walk away, a tired, headachy, light-headed or depressed feeling comes over you? Have you spent time with a group of people and come away feeling drained, bored or out of sorts? Have you noticed that spending time with certain people makes you feel on edge? Have you ever remarked to a friend, "Well, I certainly didn't enjoy that movie! Too much violence for my taste!" Or, have you come away from an event, party, dinner at a restaurant or a date feeling that you have simply wasted your time?

And have you ever noticed that your partner, your children, roommates or co-workers seem out-of-sorts? Do you notice when someone seems eager to argue or pick a fight? And can you tell when someone is angry, frustrated or sad? The Sage and Smudge rituals we talk about in this chapter are wonderful exercises in personal clearing, personal healing work on the emotional, psychological and spiritual levels. And they are excellent tools for blessing, clearing and sharing on these levels with the people you care about. These rituals are offered as simple "guides" to exploring and understanding that the realities we encounter and experience on a daily basis truly are woven into the spiritual aspect of our lives - how our lives affect our spirit, and vice versa.

A Personal Sage and Smudge Clearing ritual can help balance your energy field, lift any "cloud" of negativity and bring a sense of calm and reassurance. Many people have told me how they use Sage and Smudge rituals to help themselves find balance and a sense of personal strength and peace in their lives. Some share these rituals with the people they care about, or spend time doing Sage and Smudge Personal Clearings together. Some of the people I have talked to combine a Sage and Smudge ritual with their usual meditation or prayer practices. And some simply keep a Sage wand accessible, and light it when they think they might benefit from it. I encourage you to try some of the suggestions in this chapter, and to create your own Sage and Smudge Personal rituals to clear your own energy field, heal and nourish your own soul/spirit.

Over the years I have "collected" many Sage and Smudge rituals. Some of the rituals are performed when people feel they have encountered negativity, sadness, frustration, anxiety, stress and other challenging emotions in the course of their lives. Often the reason for a "Personal Sage and Smudge Ritual" is to clear your personal energy field, and to heal any emotional, psychological and mental conflict you are experiencing. People often perform this type of ritual in conjunction with prayer - asking for spiritual comfort, support, guidance or protection in their lives. Here are some examples of times you may benefit from carrying out a Personal Sage and Smudge ritual of your own:

- When you have, of necessity, spent time with another individual (or group of people) that has caused you to feel "tired", "depressed", or "emotionally drained".

- When you have, of necessity or by choice, spent time with another individual who is ill.
- When you have experienced the loss of a loved one.
- When you have experienced the loss of a pet.
- When you have experienced the loss (death) of a friend or someone who was important to you.
- When a friendship has ended.
- When a personal (intimate) relationship has ended.
- When you have been betrayed by someone you trusted.
- When you have been involved in an unpleasant situation at work (an altercation with a co-worker; you have been criticized for the quality of your work; you have been passed up for promotion, etc.)
- When you have been given notice that you must leave your place of employment.
- When an accident/illness/tragedy has happened at work, or to someone at work.
- When you have been involved in an altercation with a friend or a family member.
- When you (or a loved one) has been the victim of a crime.
- When you have been involved in an unpleasant experience with an authority figure (for example, you may have received a ticket for a moving violation, been to court in the course of a legal matter or been audited by the IRS).
- When you have witnessed something very unpleasant, such as a crime against others, or some

kind of physical or emotional violence or abuse between others (whether you know them or they are strangers).

- When you have been involved in an accident or inadvertently caused harm to something or someone else.
- When you or someone you care about are diagnosed with a serious disease or chronic condition.
- When you or someone you care about are diagnosed with a life-threatening illness.
- When you feel ill and know that your physical symptoms reflect an emotional or psychological reality going on inside of you.
- When you feel surrounded by "negativity", or feel "victimized" by circumstance for any reason.

To think about...

Sometimes you will simply want to perform a "quick" Personal Sage and Smudge ritual when you return home from work. Some people Sage and Smudge themselves every day when they arrive home, and others carry out a simple ritual after a particularly stressful day. It can even be a good idea to carry out this type of simple ritual when you return home after a stressful, unpleasant or unsatisfying meeting or date!

Sometimes people carry out a Personal Sage and Smudge ritual in celebration of events that happen in their lives as well. In Chapter 3 you will find lists of a variety of times (based on the cycles of the Moon) when people commonly carry out Sage and Smudge rituals of all kinds - both in celebration of a new opportunity or experience, or to clear and heal situations like the ones we all encounter along our path through life.

Tips and Tools

When you perform a Personal Sage and Smudge Clearing, it might be a good idea to use a combination of herbs. You can choose from the abbreviated list below, or refer to Chapter 1 for more information about the qualities and historical use of various herbs. You may also want to combine an herbal smudge ceremony with burning incense, lighting scented candles, or taking a scented warm bath (followed by the application of herbal lotions to your body). All of these personal rituals create a spiritual sense of harmony and peace in your life. They help you to focus on the good and wonderful things that happen on your journey through the day, and they help to heal the effects of meeting the many challenges each of us encounters along the path of life.

Desert Sage: Use to drive out negativity and the energy of negative others with whom you have been in contact. Commonly used as a smudge to purify people and places before other ceremonies take place (in the American Indian tradition).

White Sage: Use this herb as you would Desert Sage. It has a somewhat "sweeter" aroma when it is used as a smudge.

Cedar: Use to purify. This herb is especially known and valued for its ability to ease negative emotions of all kinds.

Copal: According to the ancient Mayans, Copal was believed to be a "food of the Gods" and that any prayers they prayed while burning this substance would "go directly to the ear of god." You can substitute **Frankincense** for this resin.

Juniper: Use this herb to create a safe place for yourself, and for those you care about. Traditionally people carried a bit of this herb in a little "medicine pouch" or in their pockets to protect them from harm in the course of their daily lives.

Lavender: This herb is most often used to bring a peaceful, relaxed feeling. It is also known for restoring balance and creating a sense of peace. According to tradition it draws loving energy, angels and spirits to support us.

Mugwort: Use this herb to increase your intuition and to remember your dreams. The Lakota Sioux believe that burning this herb causes negativity to leave a person's aura or energy field.

Rosemary: Use this herb for the purposes of attracting friendship and love and to drive away fear.

Thyme: Use this herb when you need courage and to improve friendships.

Quick Personal Sage and Smudge Ritual:

Most of the time, all you need is a few minutes to clear and heal your personal space and your energy field. You may want to do something as simple as placing a small White Sage Wand, a feather and some matches on a ceramic plate inside the front door (or whatever door you enter as you come home). When you enter your personal "sanctuary", your home, you can light the wand. As the smoke starts to rise, hold the wand in your left hand (if you are right-handed) and with the feather in the other hand, fan the smoke towards you.

Direct it first towards your heart, then up towards your face and the top of your head. Imagine a circle around you, and smudge down the right side of your body towards your right foot. Smudge first the right foot, then the left foot and continue upwards, fanning the smoke up the left side of your body. At the head and shoulders once again, use the feather to waft the smudge behind your back. Picture or visualize the smudge touching, almost "washing" every part of your body (and your aura), and clearing any stressful vibrations surrounding you. Sacred smoke enfolds you, clearing all the stress experienced during the day, and healing your personal energy field from top to toe.

As you waft the sacred smoke towards yourself, say: "Peace and safety, comfort and love surround me. I am safe, secure and protected here." Repeat the affirmation three times, then tap the burning end of the Sage wand against the plate until the smoke stops rising and any embers have stopped burning. Leave the wand on the plate, and check back 10-15 minutes later to make sure that your smudge stick is "out".

You may have a similar "Quick Sage and Smudge Personal ritual" that you perform before going to bed, at the time you pay your bills, clean your home, or bring home the groceries. Simple, quick, Personal Sage and Smudge rituals remind us that we are committed and connected to our spirituality on a regular basis.

Full Personal Sage and Smudge Clearing and Healing Ritual

When you plan a full Personal Sage and Smudge Clearing and Healing ritual, carefully select a time when you know you will not be interrupted. Be sure you can take all the time you need to cleanse, clear and heal any negativity that may surround you. Plan to allow yourself enough time for the ritual itself, and for a "sacred meal" or other pleasant activity afterward. You will feel relaxed after your ritual - and it is very likely you will sleep deeply or dream intensely when you have taken the time to experience your own Full Sage and Smudge Clearing and/or Healing Ceremony. For this reason, it might be a good idea to plan the event in the evening, or when you know you will have time for at least a short "nap" following your ritual.

As you gather your tools for the ritual and clothe yourself comfortably, you may want to prepare something to drink during the ceremony - some fresh water, or a favorite tea (or juice) would be perfect. If you like journaling, have your journal and some pens or pencils available. Place some favorite possessions around you in the room. Put on some music if you like, light candles (or scented candles) and set the lighting in the room to create the ambience that pleases you most.

Before you start burning your Sage and Smudge, sit quietly and think about the reason you are creating this "sacred space", this "prayer time" or "meditation time" in your life. Think about any challenges you are facing, any emotional difficulties, or problems that have been worrying you. Also, take some time and think about the good things in your life, the "happy moments" of your days, people, pets and happenings that have brought joy into your life. And especially, think about your hopes and wishes for the future! If you like, you can write down some of your thoughts in your journal, and compare them with the thoughts that will come to mind during and after your Personal Sage and Smudge ritual.

You can use a Sage wand or a combination wand for your personal ritual, but most people find it easier to combine loose leaves of Sage (White Sage) and other herbs in a vessel or container they use specifically for this type of ritual. If you are going to use loose herbs, have additional ones within easy reach, in case you want to add more to your smudge vessel. And it is a good idea to have additional matches or a lighter nearby so you can re-light the herbs you are burning as necessary.

Place the herbs you have selected in a shell, vessel or container you use for Personal Sage and Smudge rituals. Place the vessel on a fire-resistant surface - preferably on the floor in the middle of the room where you are performing the ritual. Light the herbs carefully with a match, and as they begin to burn and create the sacred smoke for your ritual, the essence of the herbs will clear the physical, emotional, spiritual and psychological levels of your being (also known as your body and your aura or "energy field"). You may want to use a feather or a fan to move the smoke around your body as it rises from the vessel.

Start your ritual with a prayer thanking the spirit world for its protection, support and love. With your feather (or fan), waft the smoke upwards towards the heavens. Waft the smoke symbolically in the four directions - North, East, South and West - as you express gratitude for the good things going on in your life. Then thank "Mother Earth" for providing shelter, comfort and support to you in your physical reality as you move the smoke towards your feet. Now you can proceed, fanning the smoke around your body in the manner described in the brief ceremony above, or in the following way:

"Cup" the smoke in your hands and bring it towards your body with your hands. First bring it towards the top of your head - asking that your mind may think clearly. Then move it towards your eyes, asking that your eyes may see and recognize what is important in your life. Bring the smoke to your mouth, jaw and throat, asking that you may speak truthfully and that your words be of comfort and worth to all who hear them.

"Bathe" your extremities in the smudge as well. As you do so, ask that your shoulders, arms and hands be strong enough (and quick enough) to carry the burdens and perform the tasks required of them. Ask for the healing you need at all levels of your being (physical, psychological, emotional and spiritual); and ask that you remain strong and healthy. Then as you gently touch your torso, hips and thighs, ask that you be blessed, that your back be guarded and protected, and that your legs and feet carry you forward along the pathway of your life's journey bringing to you the experiences, places and people who will provide the learning, love and support your soul needs.

Finally, cup the smoke and pull it towards your heart, asking that love surround you, that you be willing to both give and receive love from those who are part of your life now, those who will be part of your life in the future - those with whom you will share your experience of living.

You may want to 'walk over" the smoke at some point during your ritual, as the woman in the introduction to this chapter did. In that case, step back and forth across the rising smudge a few times, allowing the sacred smoke energy to touch your body from all sides. (Be careful with any loose clothing! Do not allow them to get too close to the embers burning in your smudge vessel!)

This process helps you to "focus your energy" inward. Now you are ready to commune with yourself - body, mind and spirit at one with the Whole. Think the thoughts you were planning to think as you prepared for the ritual, ponder the possibilities your life has to offer, and ask for the help you need to accomplish the tasks or reach the goals you desire. Or you can simply ask for resolution/ guidance in situations that are challenging to you now. Trust that resolution and the answers you need are on the way.

Most often people experience a very powerful spiritual connection with God, The Universe, Energy, Angels, Guides, The Great Spirit, Buddha (however they personally perceive the world of Spirit) during a ritual of this nature. Many ideas and thoughts come to them, in answer to the questions they may have. Allow yourself to sit and think, meditate, relax and commune with Spirit for a time.

When you are finished with this ritual, you can either allow the herbs to continue smudging until they finish burning on their own, or you can pour sand into the vessel to put out any remaining embers. Now is a good time to write your thoughts in your journal, set goals for the future, plan activities that benefit you on many levels - or simply eat a good meal or take a relaxing bath before sleeping.

Other Personal Sage and Smudge Rituals

Sometimes, in the process of one Sage and Smudge Clearing, you become aware that the feelings you are experiencing during the ritual are not what you had expected before you started! The thoughts and feelings you become aware of may be more about the people in your life, situations you have encountered, or memories and experiences from the past. Or perhaps you are still grieving over the loss of someone you loved. (Grief can also arise from other kinds of circumstances; losses of all kinds are unfortunately often a part of our lives.) Or you feel anger, frustration, sadness, regret, guilt - strong emotions you realize have nothing to do with the ritual you planned.

When this happens, finish the Sage and Smudge Clearing you have started. Then move into another room, and prepare a separate sacred smoke ceremony to clear and resolve this issue, to heal your own mind, body and spirit. Use a different Sage and Smudge wand or stick than the one you have used for the first clearing. Or prepare a fresh assortment of loose Sage and herbs to burn in a fresh Sage and Smudge vessel for this "Personal Clearing".

If the thoughts and feelings that arose involve another person, find a picture or something that represents them to be part of the Sage and Smudge ritual you are going to carry out. If the thoughts and feelings involve a situation from the past, find a memento of it (perhaps a piece of clothing you were wearing, some shoes, a "souvenir") - or open your journal or diary to anything you may have written about the event. If you are grieving, or experiencing some other strong emotion, select one of your possessions that reminds you of the person or situation causing this feeling, and bring it into the room to be part of your Sage and Smudge Healing ritual.

Begin the Sage and Smudge Healing ritual by lighting the wand or the loose herbs. The purpose of this process is to smudge your energy field, and to clear the relationship or the memory of any negative energy, and to heal your own spirit in the context of this experience. You want to leave any unhappiness behind, and go forward into the future with a feeling of optimism and hopefulness - without the entanglement of past experiences blocking your way - either in the context of your relationship, your experience of or response to an event.

As the smoke begins to rise, wait a few moments to make sure that it will continue to do so. When the wand or herbs are smudging thickly, use your hands and your breath to move the smoke towards the heavens, asking the Creator: "Heal and protect my spirit from all harm, all anger, all sadness, all fear, all negative energy." Then fan or move the smoke in each of the four directions, facing them in turn: North, East, South and West. As you face each direction, move the sacred smoke in that direction as you repeat this affirmation.

Clear the "person", the "memory" or strong emotion by fanning the smoke in a clockwise motion - to symbolize the healing energy of "time" - around the object that represents them. If you are healing a relationship, talk out loud, as if to the person (as if they were in the room with you) about the situation that has created negativity in the relationship. If you are healing the memory of a past experience, talk out loud to Spirit and express your feelings, your considerations, your fears, your regrets, your anger or frustration; speak of all that is affecting your peace of mind in the present.

If you are grieving a loss, you may wish to affirm that you continue to feel thankfulness for the opportunity you had to enjoy the people or the circumstances now no longer part of your life. If you have lost someone dear to you, affirm that you are grateful for the time you were able to share with one another on this earth; and affirm that you continue to feel gratitude and love for the spirit of your loved one. If you have lost a "way of life", affirm that you are grateful for the time you were able to spend, the learnings you recognize have improved your life, and the opportunity you had to be part of that experience. Acknowledge how important the people or the lessons were to you, and how important they will be to you in the future.

Then raise both hands to the heavens, and lower them to "cup" some of the smudge and bring it towards your heart, affirming: "I am safe and secure, protected and nurtured by Spirit and all of the loving energies of the heavens and this earth. I understand and forgive the past. I deserve love, respect and happiness. I am open to all benefit. I accept healing (in this relationship, or in this life lesson...). I accept happiness. I accept joy." Repeat this affirmation four times as you face each of the directions in turn: North, East, South and West. Then conclude with your own prayer to the Creator.

Stand still for a moment, consciously breathing in the scent of the "Sacred Smoke." Visualize power, positive energy and love filling each cell in your body. Imagine power, positive energy, strength and a feeling of harmony surrounding the very essence of your being at this moment. Visualize yourself surrounded by the light of your spirit and of your own glowing energy field. Feel the power and resilience of your spirit. When you are ready, put out the Sage wand or the Sage and Smudge herbs in the way you normally do. Following such an intense ritual, it is a good idea to spend a little time in contemplation or meditation - or write your thoughts in your journal.

Illustration by Dawn Mathews

101 Personal Sage and Smudge Rituals

1. *Clear and heal your personal space*
2. *Celebrate and Affirm positive changes in your life*
3. *Moving into a new home*
4. *Moving into a new apartment*
5. *Starting a new job*
6. *Starting a new project*
7. *Opening a bank account*
8. *Dating a new person*
9. *Buying a new car*
10. *Buying a new wardrobe*
11. *Having a make-over*
12. *Starting a diet*
13. *Starting a new health regime*
14. *Starting an exercise program*
15. *Arrival of a new pet*
16. *Celebrate the birth of a child*
17. *Celebrate the beginning of a New Year*
18. *Celebrate a birthday*
19. *Re-decorating your home or apartment*

29. *Following a Feng Shui consultation in your home*
30. *Following a Feng Shui consultation in your place of business*
31. *Repair your home*
32. *Complete re-design of your living space*
33. *Following home improvements*

34. Expand your area of expertise through study
35. Expand your work responsibilities
36. Seek a promotion
37. Expand your customer base
38. Promotional activities (such as advertising campaigns)
39. Increase business
40. Increase income (or seek a raise)
41. Assume more responsibility in a club or organization you belong to
42. Improve your current relationships
43. Explore investment opportunities
44. Promote or participate in a cause
45. Legal action against another party
46. Defend legal action against yourself
47. Sell a home
48. Sell a vehicle
49. Garage Sale
50. Offer your resignation
51. End a relationship
52. File divorce papers
53. Serve divorce papers
54. Leave one home or area to move to another
55. Leave home for college
56. Start living on your own
57. Finishing school
58. Join 12-step programs
59. Stop smoking
60. Clear clutter

61. *Remove negative energy*
62. *Remove stressful situations from your life*
63. *Remove stressful people from your life*
64. *Give up bad habits of any kind.*
65. *Last payment on a credit card*
66. *Last payment on a vehicle*
67. *Last day at a specific job*
68. *Retirement*
69. *Children going off to college*
70. *Children leaving home*
71. *Letting go of pets*
72. *Clear sleeplessness*
73. *Clear compulsive behaviors*
74. *Clear stress*
75. *Let go of anger and resentment*
76. *Ask for wisdom and understanding*
77. *Ask to know an answer*
78. *Ask for peace*
79. *Clear negative energy in your entire home*
80. *Clear negative energy in your bedroom*
81. *Clear negative energy in your garage*
82. *Clear negative energy in the vehicle you drive*
83. *Clear negative energy in your family*
84. *Clear negative energy in your environment*
85. *Clear negative energy in your kitchen*
86. *Clear negative energy in your home office*
87. *Clear negative energy where you work*
88. *Clear negative energy in your relationships*
89. *Clear negative energy from objects*

90. Clear negative energy from gifts/presents you receive

91. Clear energy fields and auras

92. Clear and support healing in emotional issues

93. Clear and support healing of psychological blocks

94. Clear and support healing in challenging relationships

95. Clear and support healing from loss or grief

96. Clear and your healing from issues out of your past

97. Enhance celebrations of joy in your life

98. Celebrate a new beginning in your life

99. Celebrate increasing physical, psychological, emotional and spiritual well-being

100. Celebrate a new opportunity

101. Celebrate and affirm your connection to Spirit.....

BIBLIOGRAPHY

Plant Folklore published by Geddes & Grosset

The Herb Book by John Lust

Encyclopedia of Native American Shamanism - Sacred Ceremonies of North America by William S. Lyon

Sage & Smudge - Secrets of Clearing Your Personal Space by Donna Stellhorn

Trees for Healing - Harmonizing with Nature for Personal Growth and Planetary Balance by Pamela Louise Chase & Jonathan Pawlik

Buffalo Woman Comes Singing by Brooke Medicine Eagle

Reader's Digest of American Folklore and Legend 1978, Pleasantville, NY

Encyclopedia of Magical Herbs by Scott Cunningham

Earth Power by Scott Cunningham

The Herb Society of America Encyclopedia of Herbs by D. Brown, 1995

Color - A Secret Language Revealed by Diane Ronngren

Funk and Wagnall's Standard Dictionary of Folklore, Mythology and Legend by M. Leach

Oregon State University Master Gardener Program http://www.orst.edu/extension

Indiana State University www.ipm.istate.edu/hortnews

http://www.herbweb.com

http://www.lavenderfarm.com/history.htm

http://countrycottageworks.com

http://home.att.nel/~waeshael/folklore.htm

http://www.herbweb.com

About Diane Ronngren

Author Diane Ronngren enjoys helping people make the connection between the practical realities of life, and the spiritual journey of the soul. She looks at life from an unusual perspective; "Every pursuit - business, career, prosperity, relationships, spirituality, happiness, personal growth - is part of the flow of energy in your life. Each day presents new avenues of discovery; opportunities for greater success and satisfaction and the expression of your gifts in the world. Life's journey must be fun, it can be challenging; and if it's exciting and rewarding, all the better!"

With degrees in business and languages, advanced certification in Astrology, Eriksonian Hypnosis and NLP, Diane is able to approach the many aspects of life with both understanding and common sense. Communication of all kinds - preferably traceable to antiquity and custom - is her special area of interest. Currently a writer, consultant and lecturer, she previously pursued careers in adult education, international corporate management, and diplomacy. Since 1988 she has expressed many of her gifts through her own business. Her work is widely recognized, and she personally teaches and mentors other Astrology and Metaphysical professionals.

Now Diane is comfortably settled in Reno, Nevada, after many years spent overseas, in Southern California and New Mexico. When she is not busy with her work she enjoys helping her husband, Gary, with their publishing company, maintaining a comfortable home and relaxing with the people and pets they love.

Diane Ronngren is available for consultations, workshops, seminars and speaking engagements.

You can contact her at: diane@etcpublishing.com